Postmortem

DATE DUE			

1. Nicola Sacco. (Courtesy Boston Public Library)

2. Bartolomeo Vanzetti. (Courtesy Boston Public Library)

POSTMORTEM

New Evidence in the Case of
Sacco and Vanzetti
William Young and David E. Kaiser

The University of Massachusetts Press / Amherst 1985

Copyright © 1985 by The University of Massachusetts Press

All rights reserved

Printed in the United States of America

Second printing

Library of Congress Cataloging in Publication Data

Young, William, 1927–1980.

Postmortem: new evidence in the case of Sacco

and Vanzetti.

Bibliography: p.

Includes index.

1. Sacco-Vanzetti case. 2. Trials (Murder)—

Massachusetts—Dedham. I. Kaiser, David E., 1947–

II. Title.

KF224.S2Y68   1985   345.73'02523   84-24483

ISBN 0–87023–478–1   347.3052523

ISBN 0–87023–479–X (pbk.)

For Dorothy Young, Stanley Oldfield, Jr., and Steve Flink

Contents

Illustrations

Preface

This book has a curious history. The late William Young of Wellesley, Massachusetts, was a highly successful rare book and art dealer and the editor of the *Dictionary of American Artists, Painters, and Sculptors.* His success gave him ample time to pursue other interests. In 1977 I was introduced to him by Steve Flink, a mutual friend staying at his house for a weekend. Most of the conversation that day dealt with tennis, a passion we all shared. Then, as I was leaving, I noticed on his bookshelf the five thick volumes of the record of the trial of Sacco and Vanzetti. Having read something about the case myself, I asked him if he was interested in it.

I had stumbled upon a man who had spent more than ten years researching every aspect of the case. His knowledge far outstripped mine, and his conclusions were, to say the least, surprising. A few weeks later he secured a copy of the Massachusetts State Police files released after the fiftieth anniversary of the execution of Sacco and Vanzetti, and began a new phase of his research. We rapidly became friends, and I became the sounding board for his new conclusions. He began preparing a manuscript embodying his findings, and we sometimes spoke about the possibility of working on it together. But having just begun a career as a university history teacher I was too busy with other projects, and nothing ever came of this idea. He eventually completed a manuscript but recognized that it was not in finished form.

In January 1980 William Young, then fifty-two years old, was stricken with terminal cancer. I found him in remarkably good spirits on my last visit to him. We agreed that I would take the manuscript and the documentation he had collected and try to put it into publishable form. He died in April 1980. My work on the manuscript received a tremendous boost when my new employer, the History and Philosophy Department of Carnegie-Mellon University, provided funding for more research. With the help of Michael Levitin and Catherine Hustead, I developed a great deal of new material and broadened the scope of the manuscript. I must thank Mrs. Erika Chadbourne of the Harvard Law School Library, the staff of the Boston Public Library, Donald Smith and Keith Halsey of the Federal Bureau of Investigation, and Susan Falb of the National Archives for their help in leading me to many important documents on the case. I must also thank Catherine Casey of the Massachusetts Supreme

Judicial Court archive for permission to duplicate several photographs of the scene of the crime; Professor Regis Pelloux of M.I.T. for his technical help; and Massachusetts Commissioner of Public Safety Frank Trabucco.

What follows is a true collaborative effort. On the one hand, it reflects both authors' conclusions; on the other, neither author would ever have produced it by himself. The authors discussed its most important conclusions at great length; they did not differ on any fundamental point, and I am certain that the book contains nothing that either one could take exception to. We intended to help clear up one of the longest, bitterest, and most fascinating controversies in the history of the United States.

David E. Kaiser

Postmortem

1 / Introduction

WHEREAS: A half century ago next month, Nicola Sacco and Bartolomeo Vanzetti were executed by the Commonwealth of Massachusetts after being indicted, tried and found guilty of murdering Alessandro Berardelli and Frederick A. Parmenter; and

WHEREAS: Nicola Sacco and Bartolomeo Vanzetti were Italian immigrants who lived and worked in Massachusetts while openly professing their beliefs in the doctrines of anarchism; and

WHEREAS: The atmosphere of their trial and appeals was permeated by prejudice against foreigners and hostility toward unorthodox political views; and

WHEREAS: The conduct of many of the officials involved in the case shed serious doubt on their willingness and ability to conduct the prosecution and trial of Sacco and Vanzetti fairly and impartially; and

.   .   .   .   .   .

WHEREAS: Simple decency and compassion, as well as respect for truth and an enduring commitment to our nation's highest ideals, require that the fate of Nicola Sacco and Bartolomeo Vanzetti be pondered by all who cherish tolerance, justice and human understanding; and

WHEREAS: Tuesday, August 23, 1977, will mark the fiftieth anniversary of the execution of Nicola Sacco and Bartolomeo Vanzetti by the Commonwealth of Massachusetts;

NOW, THEREFORE, I, Michael S. Dukakis, Governor of the Commonwealth of Massachusetts, by virtue of the authority conferred upon me as Supreme Executive Magistrate by the Constitution of the Commonwealth of Massachusetts, and by all other authority vested in me, do hereby proclaim Tuesday, August 23, 1977, "NICOLA SACCO AND

BARTOLOMEO VANZETTI MEMORIAL DAY"; and declare further, that any stigma and disgrace should be forever removed from the names of Nicola Sacco and Bartolomeo Vanzetti, from the names of their families and descendants, and so, from the name of the Commonwealth of Massachusetts; and I hereby call upon all the people of Massachusetts to pause in their daily endeavors to reflect upon these tragic events, and draw from their historic lessons the resolve to prevent the forces of intolerance, fear, and hatred from ever again uniting to overcome the rationality, wisdom, and fairness to which our legal system aspires.

It was characteristic of the case of Sacco and Vanzetti that Governor Michael Dukakis, attempting to close the episode on the fiftieth anniversary of the execution of the two men, refused to express any firm opinion regarding their guilt or innocence. For it is one of the extraordinary features of this, the most celebrated criminal case in American history, that uncertainty has increased rather than diminished in the six decades since the trial took place. As layer upon layer of evidence has gradually been uncovered, new interpretations have proliferated without ever arriving at anything like a consensus. The process was not yet complete when Governor Dukakis issued his proclamation. At almost the same moment, the Massachusetts State Police released new documentation leading to a new view of the case.

The case began in May 1920 when a local southeastern Massachusetts police chief arrested two anarchists, the shoe worker Nicola Sacco and the fish peddler Bartolomeo Vanzetti, on suspicion of two crimes. Vanzetti was immediately charged with an attempted payroll robbery in Bridgewater on 24 December 1919, and both were eventually charged with the murder of two guards, Frederick Parmenter and Alessandro Berardelli, in the successful robbery of a fifteen-thousand-dollar payroll in South Braintree on 15 April 1920. Vanzetti was tried and convicted of the Bridgewater holdup attempt in Plymouth in June and July of 1920. The case began to arouse national and international interest in the latter part of 1920, thanks largely to Fred Moore, a radical lawyer from the West Coast whom anarchists had hired to take the case.

Together with two local lawyers, J. J. McAnarney and William Callahan, Moore represented the two men when their trial for first-degree murder finally opened in Dedham on the last day of May 1921. They faced a mandatory death penalty if convicted. As in Vanzetti's earlier Plymouth trial the prosecutor was District Attorney Frederick Katzmann and the judge was Webster Thayer. During the six-week trial the prosecution presented eyewitnesses who placed Sacco and Vanzetti at or near the crime, tried to tie the two guns found on the men when arrested to the murder, and argued that their behavior on the night of their arrest indicated their guilt. The defense relied mainly on other eyewitnesses who denied Sacco and Vanzetti had taken part in the crime and on alibi witnesses for both men. The jury found both men guilty of murder in the first degree.

During the next few years the defense filed several motions for a new trial based upon new evidence. Judge Thayer, who by law had to rule on all these motions, denied five of them in October of 1924. By that time Fred Moore had left the defense after numerous quarrels with the anarchist-organized defense committee over money and a violent personal dispute with Sacco. He was replaced by William G. Thompson, a prominent Yankee lawyer who came to regard the case as a critical test of the institutions in which he had always believed.

In late 1925, while appeals of the various defense motions were pending before the Supreme Judicial Court, a new factor was introduced into the case. Another convicted murderer, one Celestino Madeiros, confessed to having participated in the South Braintree robbery and murder in a party that did not include either Sacco or Vanzetti. Although Madeiros refused to name his confederates, his story led another defense attorney, Herbert Ehrmann, directly to the Morelli gang of Providence, Rhode Island. During 1926 Ehrmann built an extraordinary circumstantial case against the Morellis, even discovering that some police officers had suspected them of the South Braintree crime at the time it took place. But Thayer again denied a motion for a new trial based on this evidence in October 1926.

By this time interest in the case was reaching unprecedented heights. Communist and other left-wing groups made it a cause célèbre in Europe and all over the world, and American liberals, whose favorite journals, the *Nation* and the *New Republic*, had always followed the case with interest, began to regard the two men's innocence as an article of faith. Publicity escalated with the publication in the March 1927 *Atlantic Monthly* of "The Case of Sacco and Vanzetti" by Harvard law professor and future Supreme Court justice Felix Frankfurter, who passionately argued the two men's innocence and the unfairness of their trial. Undeterred, the Massachustts Supreme Judicial Court also denied the motion for a new trial based on the Morelli evidence in April 1927, and Judge Thayer immediately imposed the death sentence on Sacco and Vanzetti.

The two men's fate now seemed to rest with Governor Alvan T. Fuller, a self-made millionaire automobile salesman. But after some hesitation Fuller took the unprecedented step of appointing Harvard President A. Lawrence Lowell, M.I.T. President Samuel W. Stratton, and Massachusetts Judge Robert Grant to a three-man advisory committee. In June and July the committee heard new evidence. It concluded that the original trial was fair and that the two men were guilty. Fuller endorsed this decision and denied clemency on 3 August 1927. After three additional weeks of frantic appeals the two men were executed shortly after midnight on 23 August 1927, amidst enormous demonstrations all over the world. Passion was not confined to one side; such was the strength of conservative establishment feeling against the two men and their supporters that movie czar Will Hays ordered the destruction of all copies of the film of their gigantic funeral procession through Boston.

It was primarily the political overtones of the case that had made it into one of the great international controversies of the age. Left-wingers and liberals believed the two men had been singled out for their beliefs and their ancestry. It became an article of faith that the two poor Italian anarchists had stood no chance at the hands of the bigoted Yankees who stocked the Massachusetts judiciary, the Lowell Committee, and, for that matter, the jury. Judge Thayer, who was found to have made some violently prejudiced remarks about the defendants during the various proceedings, became a symbol of bigoted justice. On the other side, respectable opinion increasingly believed that Communists had made international heroes out of two bandits to whom the court system and Governor Fuller had given extraordinary opportunities to prove their innocence. At the same time, politics would not have sufficed to make the case so controversial had not the facts of the case, as known at the time, allowed for belief in either their innocence or their guilt. By 1927 firearms evidence had told heavily against Sacco. Thus Walter Lippmann, then a *New York World* editorial writer, had initially enraged many liberal friends, including Frankfurter, by refusing to blast the Lowell Committee's report. One reason, his letters now show, was that he suspected Sacco's involvement. The same ambivalence was apparent in Upton Sinclair's huge novel, *Boston*, which clearly drew a distinction between the two defendants and refused unequivocally to assert Sacco's innocence. Even Fred Moore expressed serious doubts as to Sacco's innocence after his angry exchanges with Sacco had led to his departure from the case.

Still, for more than twenty years published studies of the case generally supported the hypothesis of Sacco and Vanzetti's innocence. A massive 1931 study by Osmond K. Fraenkel, *The Sacco-Vanzetti Case*, leaned strongly toward such a conclusion, as did a New York attorney, Edmund M. Morgan, in *The Legacy of Sacco and Vanzetti*, which he coauthored with G. Louis Joughin in 1948. In the meantime Herbert Ehrmann brilliantly elaborated the Morelli theory in *The Untried Case*, which appeared in 1934. By the 1950s most educated people clearly believed Sacco and Vanzetti to have been innocent victims, but the Commonwealth of Massachustts declined to repudiate its proceedings. A 1959 effort to persuade the legislature to grant the men a posthumous pardon was a dismal failure.

The 1960s showed that the case still stirred considerable feeling. In 1960 a Boston attorney, Robert Montgomery, published *Sacco-Vanzetti: The Murder and the Myth*. Though essentially a restatement of the prosecution's case, it was still the first full-length study to argue the defendants' guilt. Two years later, in 1962, came the real bombshell, Francis Russell's monumental *Tragedy in Dedham*. Thoroughly researching the case, Russell combined a skillful re-creation of the crime, trial, and subsequent agitation with accounts of his own more recent investigations, including interviews with some survivors of the actual proceedings. Most significantly, he persuaded the Massachusetts State Police to authorize new firearms tests involving the Colt automatic found on Sacco and one of the bullets introduced at the trial as having come from one of the murdered guards. He concluded, based on these tests, that Sacco was guilty. He exonerated Vanzetti on largely subjective grounds, although he subsequently argued that the revolver found upon him was probably taken from Berardelli during the robbery. David Felix's 1965 book, *Protest: Sacco-Vanzetti and the Intellectuals*, did not systematically analyze the evidence but seemed to believe that the two men were guilty as well. Then in 1969 Herbert Ehrmann's *The Case That Will Not Die* marshaled the case for the defense as thoroughly as Montgomery and Russell had put the case for the prosecution. The Commonwealth of Massachusetts, however, did not permit Ehrmann to retest the firearms evidence, as Russell had done eight years earlier.

The 1970s were quieter, though Russell continued to elaborate his position in magazine articles and in an introduction to a new edition of his book. But the fiftieth anniversary of Sacco and Vanzetti's execution in 1977 was the occasion for a further reopening of the case. A new book, Roberta Strauss Feuerlicht's *Justice Crucified*, argued once again on behalf of the defendants' innocence, although without introducing any new material or stating its case with any particular sophistication. The impact of recent debates was clearly visible in "The Never-Ending Wrong," Katherine Anne Porter's account of her activities as a protester in 1927 in the *Atlantic*. Miss Porter restated her commitment to the defendants' cause but concluded with an admission that Russell had persuaded her that Sacco might quite possibly have been guilty. More important, Massachustts Governor Michael Dukakis issued his proclamation regarding Sacco and Vanzetti. Angry protests from descendants of some of those involved, including children of Governor Fuller, proved once again that the case was more than a matter of academic interest.

The renewal of the controversy coincided with the release of large amounts of new documentation relating to the case. On the whole, every book written on the case since Fraenkel had been based upon the same basic source: the six volumes of trial record published in 1928 by Henry Holt, including the transcript of the trial, the mass of evidence developed by the defense in support of various appeals, the transcript of Vanzetti's Plymouth trial, and the proceedings of the Lowell Committee.[1] In 1977, however, the Massachusetts State Police released an enormous file on the case in response to a Freedom of Information Act suit brought by Lincoln Robbins. The file included copies of inquiries addressed to the Commonwealth since the execution of the two men; an enormous transcript of conversations recorded by a listening device placed on the telephone of Felix Frankfurter, then a Harvard law professor and defense advocate; and reports from a police informer who had penetrated the defense committee. Most important of all, it included critical material on the development of the prosecution's case before the trial.

Since 1977 other material of ever greater importance has been discovered at the Harvard Law School Library, including the minutes of the hitherto secret grand jury proceedings and the notebooks of Harold Williams, the assistant district attorney who presented the prosecution's case. Important papers belonging to the defense have been opened at both the Harvard Law Library and the Boston Public Library. Researchers may now trace the preparation of both the prosecution and the defense and make use of much critical information that was never presented at the trial. In addition, numerous federal files have been opened —files that detail the government's campaign against the anarchist group to which Sacco and Vanzetti belonged and the ways in which that campaign led to their arrest for murder.

The story of the trial and subsequent agitation has been told and retold many times, but the critical issue of the defendants' guilt or innocence has remained unresolved. This new material helps to clear it up. It tells how and why Sacco and Vanzetti were arrested and what role their anarchist beliefs played in their trial for murder. It shows how the prosecution prepared its case and impeaches the testimony of numerous prosecution witnesses. Most important of all, it sheds new light on what has always been the most telling evidence against the two men: the two guns found upon them on the night of their arrest. Taken together it leads to the conclusion that Sacco and Vanzetti, two innocent men, most probably were framed for a murder they did not commit.

2 / Anarchism and the Arrests

Almost from the moment of their arrest in May 1920, the issue of antiradical or antialien prejudice has clouded the controversy over the guilt or innocence of Sacco and Vanzetti. From the beginning their defenders saw them as victims of prevailing hysteria and bigotry whom the Massachusetts judiciary could not possibly judge fairly. Such, indeed, is the theme of the two most recent books on the case.[1] Judge Thayer's antiradical prejudice has long been a matter of record, and we shall see that he had spoken out strongly against anarchism even before the trial, but for the most part he carefully kept any prejudice out of the trial record, exhorting the jury to judge the defendants as if their forefathers had sailed on the *Mayflower*. A federal agent of Italian descent who attended the first week of the trial reported intense anti-Italian feeling in the courtroom, but one cannot tell whether such feeling affected the jury.[2] Direct evidence of prejudice among the twelve Dedham jurymen that convicted Sacco and Vanzetti of murder is contradictory and inconclusive. One defense motion for a new trial included an affidavit from a Quincy contractor, William Daly, relating a conversation he had at the beginning of the trial with the since deceased jury foreman, a retired policeman named Walter Ripley. When Daly expressed his belief in the two men's innocence, Ripley replied, "Damn them, they ought to hang them anyway."[3] But other jurors strongly asserted their freedom from bias in talks with Governor Fuller and with a newspaper reporter thirty years later, and the juror John Dever, who later became an attorney, emphatically denied any prejudice in a manuscript he wrote about the case in the 1950s. And just as contemporary pamphleteers and authors like Feuerlicht and Brian Jackson have seemed to suggest that the existence of prejudice in some sense proves the two men innocent, others like Francis Russell and Robert Montgomery have implied that evidence of a lack of prejudice indicates their guilt.

In fact, the issue of prejudice must to some extent be separated from that of the defendants' guilt or innocence. An impartial jury can err, and a prejudiced one can stumble upon the truth. We can neither convict nor exonerate Sacco and Vanzetti because of their beliefs or because of the unpopularity of their beliefs; our ultimate judgment must rest upon more specific evidence. Yet, in another sense, their anarchist affiliations and the climate of the times in which they lived do have an essential bearing upon the case. For while they may or may not have been *convicted* of murder because of their political beliefs, they were undoubtedly *arrested* because of them. Their arrest on the night of 5 May 1920 resulted from a long chain of circumstances involving the political climate of the First World War, a federal campaign against radicalism, the terrorist activities of the anarchist faction to which they belonged, and the antianarchist beliefs of the chief of police, Michael Stewart, who arranged for their arrest.

The era of the First World War and its aftermath ranks with the late 1790s, the Civil War, and the Red scare of the late 1940s and early 1950s as one of the most highly politicized periods in American history. Having decided after much hesitation to enter the First World War, mainstream America quickly established a standard of absolute patriotism that left no room for dissent. The war became the occasion for attempts to submerge regional, political, and class antagonisms—all of them well established before the war—within a new, unanimous commitment to patriotic purpose. Working through the press, the educational system, and a nationwide network of seventy-five thousand "Four-Minute Men" who made themselves available for patriotic pep talks, the government indoctrinated the citizenry in the virtues of the American system and the wickedness of America's new enemies. Progressive George Creel's Committee on Public Information paid particular attention to America's millions of recent immigrants, viewing the war as an opportunity to complete the "Americanization" of alien elements.[4] Rarely if ever have Americans been subjected to such a sustained propaganda barrage, but thousands of Americans still held themselves aloof and refused to support the war.

The opposition to the war stemmed from two unrelated sources: ethnic groups either sympathetic to the Central Powers or hostile to the Allied cause, led by German- and Irish-Americans, and left-wing groups who opposed the war on principle, including the American Socialist party, the Wobblies or Industrial Workers of the World, and a host of smaller groups. Well before American entry into the war, the IWW and the American Socialists had regarded the conflict as a capitalist conspiracy against the international proletariat. They maintained their opposition in the spring of 1917. President Wilson, though generally a supporter of personal liberty and a crusader for economic democracy, had no sympathy for opponents of the war. Having persuaded himself that he was embarked upon a worldwide crusade for democracy, he expected all his fellow citizens to join in. Almost eighteen months before American entry into the war, in a December 1915 State of the Union address that called for increased preparedness, Wilson had discussed the problem of domestic disloyalty in no uncertain terms.

> I am sorry to have to say that the gravest threats against our national peace and safety have been uttered within our own borders. There are citizens of the United States, I blush to admit, born under other flags but welcomed under our generous naturalization laws to the full freedom of opportunity of America, who have poured the poison of disloyalty into the very arteries of our national life; who have sought to bring the authority and good name of our Government into contempt, to destroy our industries wherever they thought it effective for their vindictive purposes to strike at them, and to debase our politics to the uses of foreign intrigue.... A little while ago such a thing would have seemed incredible.... But the ugly and incredible thing has actually come about and we are without adequate federal laws to deal with it. I urge you to enact such laws at the earliest possible moment and feel that in so doing I am urging you to do nothing less than save the honor and self-respect of the nation. Such creatures of passion, disloyalty, and anarchy must be crushed out. They are not many, but they are infinitely malignant, and the hand of our power should close over them at once. They have formed plots to destroy property, they have entered into conspiracies against the neutrality of the Government, they have sought to pry into every confidential transaction of the Government in order to serve interests alien to our own.[5]

Indeed, Wilson secured the legislation he sought when the Espionage Act was passed in June 1917, two months after he led the country into war. Although a lengthy congressional debate had eventually removed sections bluntly giving the government the power to censor the press, the act still prescribed a ten-thousand-dollar fine and a prison sentence of up to twenty years for anyone who might "willfully cause or attempt to cause insubordination, disloyalty, mutiny, or refusal of duty in the military or naval forces of the United States, or shall willfully obstruct the recruiting or enlistment service of the United States." It also gave the Post Office the right to ban seditious literature from the mails. A controversial conscription measure had become law the month before, and the government wasted no time in seizing upon opposition to the draft as a basis for prosecuting and jailing opponents of the war under the Espionage Act. Washington did not, however, stop there. The Sedition Act of May 1918 proscribed the utterance or publication of "disloyal, profane, scurrilous, or abusive language about the form of government of the United States, or the Constitution of the United States . . . or any language intended to . . . encourage resistance to the United States, or to promote the cause of its enemies."[6]

The attack upon domestic dissent was carried out mainly by two federal agencies, the Justice Department's Bureau of Investigation and the Labor Department's Bureau of Immigration. The Bureau of Investigation—the ancestor of the FBI—had been created in 1908 without congressional approval. From its earliest days the bureau took an intense interest in leftist "radical" political groups of all kinds, including Socialists, the IWW, anarchists, and, later, the emerging American Communist party. The bureau's activity increased during the First World War, and by 1919 offices were required to submit weekly reports of radical activities within their districts.[7] The bureau received considerable assistance from an officially sponsored vigilante group, the American Protective League, which spied upon suspicious Americans, rounded up draft-age men, and tried to increase vigilance against disloyalty of all kinds. The league eventually numbered about 150,000 members.[8] The Bureau of Immigration took responsibility for alien radicals, who could be deported if they could be shown merely to advocate anarchy, the overthrow of government authority, or the destruction of property. An amended immigration act of October 1918 allowed for deportation of any alien who had *ever* held such beliefs.[9]

The biggest targets of the federal authorities' offensive were the IWW and the American Socialist party. The IWW, an avowedly revolutionary union with about 100,000 members in 1917, had actually tried to avoid provoking the government over the war. While it opposed American intervention, it did not specifically try to harm the war effort or encourage resistance to the draft. Strikes inspired by the IWW did, however, increase in the early months of the war, and in August 1917 employers and local Justice Department officials persuaded the attorney general to raid IWW offices around the country in search of evidence of a conspiracy against the war effort. Seized evidence led to the indictment of 166 IWW members on charges of obstructing the war effort through strikes and other measures and eventually to the conviction of many of them and the ruin of the organization.[10] The American Socialist party, which had polled 590,000 votes in the 1916 presidential election—about seven times its official membership—took an active stand against both the war and the draft, the only prominent national organization to do so. It rapidly paid the price. In the fall of 1917 numerous prominent Socialist publications lost their mailing privileges. In the spring of 1918 numerous Socialists were indicted and convicted under the Espionage Act. The government obtained the indictment in June of Socialist leader Eugene V. Debs.[11] Federal authorities did not, however, limit their campaign to major groups like the IWW or Socialists.

The first link in the long chain of events that led to Sacco and Vanzetti's arrest was forged in June 1917, when both the Department of Justice and the Bureau of Immigration noticed an article, "I Matricolati," in the 26 May issue of the *Cronaca Sovversiva*, an Italian anarchist periodical published in Lynn, Massachusetts, by Luigi Galleani. Addressing the question of whether aliens should register for the recently enacted draft, the article expressed opposition to the war and suggested that alien anarchists who refused to register would never be sent into the army, since the authorities would know that such men would take any opportunity to sabotage the war effort.[12] The government's interest in Galleani was aroused.

Luigi Galleani was undoubtedly one of the more romantic figures produced by the European revolutionary movement. Born in Italy in 1861, he became a bookkeeper but was arrested in Italy in 1894 for anarchist activities in opposition to a colonial war Italy was then fighting in Ethiopia. Exiled to the island of Pantelleria, he escaped and fled to Egypt a few years later, reportedly taking with him his jailer's wife, who subsequently bore him five children. He immigrated to the United States in 1901 and initially settled in Barre, Vermont, where he started his newspaper, *Cronaca Sovversiva*, in 1902. Arrested for strike activities in Barre in 1907, he was freed after a jury failed to agree. Later he was arrested on a similar charge in Donora, Pennsylvania. The *Cronaca* consistently advocated the destruction of all political, economic, and religious authority. In other writings Galleani glorified individual acts of terrorism and discussed the proper manufacture of bombs. The *Cronaca* also engaged in violent polemics against other anarchist and left-wing groups. In 1917 its subscribers included Nicola Sacco, a shoe worker living in Milford, Massachusetts, and Bartolomeo Vanzetti, who lived in Plymouth.[13]

On the basis of the article "I Matricolati," the Bureau of Immigration interrogated Galleani with a view to deportation based upon his anarchist beliefs. Galleani's first immigration hearing in June 1917 resulted in a recommendation for a deportation warrant but added that the warrant should be held in abeyance because of his large family. In August the commissioner-general of immigration sustained this recommendation, noting his opinion that a deportation order was not really justified by the evidence. Galleani, whose intelligence consistently impressed his interrogators, had generally managed to steer clear of actual advocacy of overthrow of the government in the *Cronaca Sovversiva* and had avoided any straightforward advocacy of resistance to the draft.[14]

In the meantime, Bureau of Investigation agents began a major investigation of Galleani, the *Cronaca Sovversiva*, and all its subscribers—an investigation that led them to the names of Sacco and Vanzetti. In February 1918 agents from several states took part in a raid on the *Cronaca* offices in Lynn, where they seized five thousand addresses of subscribers to the *Cronaca Sovversiva*, including those of Sacco and Vanzetti.[15] By this time several Italians closely associated with the paper had been arrested for failing to register for the draft, including David Tedesco and Rafaele Schiavine. Correspondence seized by agents in the raid on the *Cronaca* offices showed that Schiavine had fled to Monterey, Mexico, with a group of Galleanisti to avoid registering for the draft. Sacco and Vanzetti had been among them. A September 1917 letter from Monterey reported that the group was breaking up, "the reason for remaining together having failed"; "having different trades and attitudes, we cannot come together in the same way." The letter referred specifically to both Sacco and Vanzetti as two men who might return home soon; as a matter of fact, Sacco returned that very month.[16] By early 1918 the Post Office had banned the *Cronaca* from the mails, and the bureau was making a determined effort to round up a network of anarchists who were distributing it through American Express. The bureau regarded Galleani as "the leading anarchist in the United States" and described the *Cronaca* as "the largest and most dangerous anarchist newspaper published in this country."[17] Several Galleanisti were also being sought in connection with a shipment of dynamite from Connecticut to Ohio.

In May 1918 the Bureau of Immigration issued about a hundred arrest warrants for members of the Galleani or *Cronaca Sovversiva* "group," as it was customarily called. Forty of the men sought lived in the Boston area. They included Ferruccio Coacci, who eventually surrendered himself for deportation in Bridgewater on 16 April 1920, the day after the South Braintree crime; Oreste Bianchi and Giovanni Frizetti, whom

Sacco identified as friends in his trial testimony; and Vicenzo Brini, the owner of the house in Suosso's Lane, Plymouth, where Bartolomeo Vanzetti boarded before going to Mexico.[18] Immigration officials attempted to identify particularly active members of the *Cronaca* group by sifting through seized correspondence. Those singled out for arrest as anarchists had written letters or cards found by agents when they raided the paper; the bureau believed "that some are writing articles for this paper, others are taking subscriptions for it and transmitting the proceeds of same by money order, while still others are acting as distributing agents." Evidently no correspondence from either Sacco or Vanzetti was found, although seized letters from Mexico referred to both men. Thus, although Vanzetti in particular seems to have been more active than many of those marked for deportation, the two men were not on the deportation list.[19] Under the circumstances, however, they obviously must have regarded themselves as suspects liable for deportation at any time. Several of the anarchists on the list, including Ferruccio Coacci, were arrested by Chief of Police Michael Stewart of Bridgewater, whom we will meet again.[20]

Galleani himself was arrested on 16 May 1918 and interrogated anew. Boston Immigration Commissioner John Ryder still doubted that deportation was in order: "he is independent, belongs to no organization. There is no organization of anarchists in the United States any more than there is of Italian atheists." But in October the new act was passed, making it possible to deport all aliens who had ever professed anarchistic beliefs, and on 18 November—a week after the armistice in Europe—Immigration Commissioner General Anthony Caminetti recommended deportation. A new hearing resulted in a recommendation for deportation in January 1919, and after several months of legal stalling Galleani was deported on 18 June 1919.[21] A number of his followers, including Sacco and Vanzetti's friend Frizetti, were deported in the same month.

By 1919, then, the bureau's investigation of the Galleanisti had encountered the names of Sacco and Vanzetti. Sacco was also known to the Boston office of the bureau because of his radical activity in Milford. The deportation drive of the Immigration and Naturalization Service had reached several of their friends but not the two men themselves. Federal authorities were now turning their interest to the fledgling American Communist party and might well have considered the case of the Galleanisti closed had not some of Galleani's followers decided violently to protest the deportations. On 2 June 1919—several weeks *before* Galleani's deportation—bombs exploded in Pittsburgh, Philadelphia, Boston, Newtonville (Mass.), and Washington, D.C. The Washington explosion occurred directly in front of the house of the attorney general, A. Mitchell Palmer, and killed the man carrying the bomb. Several other explosions damaged the houses of judges and legislators who had been active against anarchists, and one other man, a New York watchman, was killed. A leaflet, "Plain Words," found at the site of several bombings, called for "social revolution," "class war," and "complete victory for the international proletariat" and was signed "the anarchist fighters." This obviously coordinated series of outrages created a sensation. Having escaped death or injury, Palmer turned the bombings into a godsend. Congress voted new funds for antiradical investigations, and the Bureau of Investigation, whose antisubversion mandate had lost some of its urgency since the armistice, swung into action once more.

William J. Flynn, former head of the Secret Service, became the new head of the bureau, and a nationwide investigation began. Flynn's bombing investigation eventually came under the authority of the General Intelligence Division of the Department of Justice, whose director was none other than Special Assistant to the Attorney General J. Edgar Hoover. Although many agents suspected the Galleanisti from the beginning, Galleani's deportation took place as planned in late June. For over six months agents sought to trace fragments of the dead bomber's suit, a laundry mark on his shirt, and the type of the leaflet "Plain Words," but without success. The bureau did identify a revolver found on the scene of the crime and traced its purchase to the Iver Johnson Company in Boston. Records listed its purchaser as Luigi Calisieri of 24 Wright Street, Medford, but no one by that name could be located. The Boston office searched intermittently for various Galleanisti who might have been involved but not for Sacco and Vanzetti. In the midst of their search the Newton police discovered the mailing list of the *Cronaca Sovversiva*—including the names of Sacco and Vanzetti—at a home in Newton formerly occupied by Augusto Rossi and Carlo Valdinocci. Agents heard that Galleani was now publishing the *Cronaca* in Italy, helped by donations from American anarchists said to amount to as much as twenty thousand dollars.[22] They also learned that several Galleanisti had blown themselves up attempting to set off a bomb in Franklin, Massachusetts, on 28 February 1919.[23]

The Commonwealth of Massachusetts, indeed, had at least its share of radicals, immigrants, and political and ethnic tensions, and local concern with political radicalism was high in 1919. In May of that year the legislature passed a new statute specifying up to three years' imprisonment for anyone who "by speech or by exhibition, distribution or promulgation of any written or printed document, paper or pictorial representation advocates, advises, counsels or incites assault upon any public official, or the killing of any person, or the unlawful destruction of real or personal property, or the overthrow by force or violence of the government of the commonwealth."[24] The Massachusetts House of Representatives passed the bill with only three dissenting votes, and it became law on 28 May.[25] In October a grand jury sitting in Suffolk County, in Boston, returned several indictments under this statute.[26]

Local papers in the southeastern Massachusetts towns from which the jurors in the trials of Sacco and Vanzetti would be summoned showed tremendous concern about foreign radicals. "Organized efforts are being started to fight the Bolshevistic poison. It is none too soon," the *Quincy Patriot* editorialized on 23 April 1919; three days later it stressed the need for the "Americanization" of immigrants, warning that "Naturalization does not by any means indicate Americanization" and that foreigners must be enlightened "concerning the principles and ideals of Americanism." The same editorials appeared in the *Braintree Observer* on 26 April and 3 May. "Since when has America countenanced an invasion—an incursion of foreigners hostile to Americans and American ideals?" the same paper asked on 6 May. "Our soldiers fought bravely and well at the door of the enemy; shall we, for whom they bled, continue at home to submit to the anarchist terror." Further comments on 16 May and 10 June stressed that bombers and Bolsheviks were almost all aliens. Reacting to the final passage of the law prohibiting the advocacy of anarchy, the *Norwood Messenger* of 19 June implied that the general alarm had perhaps gone too far but endorsed the punishment of those advocating acts of violence. The press consistently mixed up anarchism and bolshevism without recognizing any difference between them.

On 13 December 1919, the *Brockton Times* endorsed Tennessee Senator Kenneth McKellar's proposal to send "anarchists, bolshevists, I.W.W.'s or other Red brands" to the Philippines, where they might set up their own state. On 2 December the *Quincy Patriot* discussed the constitutional right to freedom of speech. "It seems clear that it was never intended that this provision of the Constitution should extend to permission to anarchists to advocate the destruction of government and civilization as well, and that it would apply in peace as well as in war. Liberty does not mean license, and freedom of speech should not include permission to advocate doctrines that are subversive of law and morals." A filler on the editorial page on 8 December stated, "Anarchist papers published in 25 languages in the United States furnish an equal number of reasons why English is good enough for us."

Simultaneously the Department of Justice and the Bureau of Immigration were planning a massive series of arrests of Communists all over the country preparatory to their deportation. The raids took place on 2 and 6 January 1920, and about ten thousand persons were arrested nationwide, including five hundred around Boston. Editorial reaction in southeastern Massachusetts was favorable. On 17 January a *Norwood Messenger* editorial, "The Justice of Deportation," stated, "the man who exhorts others to riot and murder, is as bad as the man who actually takes the gun and shoots." On 24 January a *Dedham Transcript* editorial approvingly quoted an 1896 speech by Henry Cabot Lodge that had discussed the danger of a "wholesale infusion of races with alien traditions and inheritances." "In dealing with these deteriorating and disrupting influences in our national life," the paper continued, "let us keep in mind the principle back of it all. This is the day of stern measures. An operation is necessary because we were lax in the past. Let us face it."

Meanwhile, both federal and state authorities were actively pursuing the perpetrators of the 2 June bombings in Boston and Newtonville. In New York an ambitious former assistant attorney general, Alfred L. Becker, who had previously made a name for himself investigating German attempts to keep the United States out of the war, enlisted the services of an Italian informant, Eugenio Ravarini. In December 1919 Ravarini traveled to New England and made contact with various anarchists, hearing at one point of an active figure named Sacco. He also stopped at the Italian Naturalization Club in Maverick Square, East Boston, a favorite hangout of both Sacco and Vanzetti. According to subsequent statements by New York anarchist Carlo Tresca, who exposed Ravarini as an informer, Ravarini consistently advocated violence and asked for the addresses of prominent Boston radicals.[27] A letter from Becker to Hoover in early March 1920, which passed on these reports, noted that "the Massachusetts investigation has been conducted at very considerable expense" and asked that Massachusets authorities remain in charge of the investigation within the Commonwealth. "The above propositions," Becker concluded, "are largely the suggestion of Governor Coolidge of Massachusetts, to whose initiative and determination to maintain the principle of law and order the undertaking in which I have been engaged is due."[28]

While Ravarini was in Massachusetts, the attempted robbery of the L. Q. White payroll took place in Bridgewater on 24 December 1919. Early in the morning, as a truck transported the sixty-thousand-dollar payroll, it encountered three bandits standing in the street, two of whom fired weapons. The truck managed to escape, and the bandits fled in a car. On that very day Bridgewater Chief of Police Michael Stewart, who had helped arrest radicals for deportation, told a Pinkerton operative assigned to the case "that he believed that the holdup was the work of an out-of-town band of Russians with a possible confederate in the White Shoe shops. As yet he said he had no clue as to who the bandits were.... The Chief said the population of Bridgewater is about 7000 persons, one third of whom are foreigners, such as Poles, Russians, Greeks, Italians, Armenians and French. He said that there are a lot of Reds and Bolshevists about town. He stated that a number of them drift in here from Connecticut and elsewhere in Massachusetts and a lot of them work for the White Company." On 30 December an informant told the Pinkertons that he had heard the crime was the work of a gang of Italian anarchists living in Quincy who had hidden the bandit car in a shack near Bridgewater, but attempts to find such a gang or such a shack did not turn up anything. When on 3 January the Pinkertons and the police interviewed the original source of this rumor—an apparent bootlegger whose appearance roughly fitted the description of one of the L. Q. White bandits—the man told a rambling story about a machine that enabled people to detect crimes but said nothing at all about anarchism. The Pinkerton investigation abruptly terminated on 9 January 1920, but Stewart's conviction that anarchists had been behind the crime remained unshaken.[29]

Federal authorities did better in their bombing investigation. In February 1920 Ravarini seems to have infiltrated a different anarchist group, the L'Era Nuova faction of Paterson, New Jersey. Federal agents arrested twenty-nine members of the group on 20 February, including its leader, Ludovico Caminiti. Questioned at Ellis Island by J. Edgar Hoover himself, Caminiti bluntly denied any complicity in the bombings but pointed the finger toward the Galleani group. He suggested that "Plain Words" might have been printed by a New York anarchist printer, Roberto Elia, and added that in October 1919 Aldino Felicani, a Galleanisti printer working in Boston, had asked him to write a manifesto justifying political direct action.[30] The tip regarding Elia led to a raid on Canzoni's print shop in Brooklyn and the discovery of the "Plain Words" type. Federal agents arrested Elia and another printer, Andrea Salsedo, in late February and early March. Given the choice of being held at the New York office of the Bureau of Investigation or going immediately to Ellis Island to await deportation, they chose the former. Elia turned out to be the anarchist printer par excellence; at different times he had printed the *Cronaca Sovversiva* in Barre, Vermont; *La Plebe*, published by the syndicalist Carlo Tresca; and *L'Era Nuova* for Caminiti in Paterson. Salsedo eventually admitted that he had printed "Plain Words" at the request of an anarchist, Nicola Recchi. Elia confirmed this.[31]

The bombing investigation now began to cross the paths of Sacco and Vanzetti. In March, New York Agent M. J. Davis went to Boston to pursue several leads. On 19 March he interrogated Aldino Felicani, a close friend of Vanzetti's.[32] Carlo Valdinocci, formerly of Somerville, had been named by several informants as a possible participant in the bombings, and in early March another agent learned that his sister Assunta had moved from Somerville to Stoughton. Another agent spent a day in Stoughton checking the post office and all the factories for signs of Assunta, but without success. Assunta may actually have been staying with the Sacco family, and the agent almost certainly stopped at the 3-K shoe factory where Sacco worked. George Kelley, Sacco's employer, told Sacco sometime early in 1920 that he (Sacco) was under investigation.[33] Davis also visited the Boston immigration office, where he learned that authorities had decided to suspend the bond of Sacco and Vanzetti's friend, Ferruccio Coacci, and deport him at the next available opportunity.[34]

Meanwhile, the Norfolk County authorities who eventually brought the case against Sacco and Vanzetti were taking antiradical measures of their own. In Norwood a Lithuanian named Sergis Zakoff had been one of hundreds of Boston radicals seized in the massive "Red Raids" against Communists on 2 January. The police found radical literature in his home, and in early 1920 the Norfolk County district attorney's office persuaded a grand jury to indict him for advocating anarchy. This decision showed unusual zeal; such prosecutions were quite uncommon. The case came to trial on 23 April 1920, just one week after the South Braintree murders. Zakoff was represented by the district attorney's brother, Percy Katzmann, and Assistant District Attorney William Kane conducted the prosecution. The judge was Webster Thayer, who had publicly vented his concern regarding anarchist propaganda at a naturalization ceremony in Dedham Courthouse just a few weeks earlier. Speaking to a large group of newly naturalized citizens, he delivered a ringing address on the rights and duties of American citizens. At one point he commented on new dangers to American values.

> Of late a new propaganda has come into our midst. It is the propaganda of force, of might and revolution, and it is prescribed as a remedy for what? For order, for obedience to law and the protection of human life. Think what that means. Oh, how unfortunate that any such a doctrine, so destructive in its character and so revolutionary in all its tendencies should ever have reached the sacred shores of these United States where the spirit of liberty and opportunity and where the freedom of person, of property and of contract are unequalled anywhere in the world.[35]

The case against Zakoff appeared to be open and shut. The statute condemned anyone who would "by speech . . . advocate, advise, counsel or incite . . . the overthrow by force or violence of the government of the commonwealth." Two police officers testified that Zakoff had told them that he was a Bolshevik, that the United States should have a revolution, and that the officers would do well to become Bolsheviks themselves. Zakoff took the stand in his own defense and avowed his views. More testimony showed that he had belonged to a Norwood club in which pictures of Russian Soviet leaders had hung upon the walls. No transcript of the trial exists, but Thayer presumably told the jury that if they believed the officers' testimony they must find Zakoff guilty. An extraordinary scene took place when the jury returned a verdict of not guilty.

"Gentlemen, how did you arrive at such a verdict?" asked Thayer.

> "Did you consider the information that the defendant gave to the police officers when he admitted, according to the three police officers, that he was a Bolshevist and that there should be a revolution in this country? Upon his own testimony he said to the officers, in the conversation they had with him, that he believed in bolshevism and that our government should be overthrown. Didn't you consider the testimony given by the police officers when you were deliberating, before you agreed on a verdict?"

In reply the foreman stated that the jury had understood the court to say that only a person who used violence, rather than one who simply talked about it, would be guilty under the statute—certainly a misinterpretation of the statute and, so far as we can see, of Thayer's own views as well. When shortly thereafter Thayer asked Kane if the Commonwealth had additional cases to present, Kane replied, "Your Honor, in view of the verdict just rendered, there is no further business today that the district attorney's office desires to try."[36]

On 15 April, in South Braintree, Massachusetts, Frederick Parmenter and Alessandro Berardelli—two employees of Slater and Morrill, a shoe factory—were attacked by two men as they carried a fifteen-thousand-dollar payroll down Pearl Street, South Braintree, at about 3:00 P.M. Both men were shot and killed, and the bandits escaped with two or three confederates who had waited in a car up the street. The state police and the Pinkertons began an immediate investigation, but it was a further chain reaction involving the continuing federal investigation of the Galleanisti and Chief Stewart's suspicions of anarchist bandits that led to the arrests of Sacco and Vanzetti. On 16 April Chief Stewart learned that the anarchist Ferruccio Coacci, whom he had believed deported long before, had failed to appear before the immigration board as scheduled the previous day, claiming his wife was sick. Coacci's deportation order had in fact resulted directly from the government's new suspicions of the Galleanisti in the June bombings. That night Stewart sent a police officer with Inspector Root of the Bureau of Immigration to see Coacci, and Coacci insisted upon leaving at once. He sailed from New York two days later. In the meantime, on Saturday, 17 April, the Buick car used in the South Braintree holdup was found in the Manley Woods, less than two miles from Puffer's Place, the house where Coacci lived. Stewart apparently remembered that Coacci had worked at L. Q. White and at Slater and Morrill and became suspicious.

Returning to Coacci's house on 20 April, Stewart met another Italian, Mike Boda. Boda, who described himself as a salesman of Italian foods, voluntarily showed Stewart around the house and the shack behind it, where his Overland car, now being repaired, was generally kept. In response to a question, Boda confirmed that Coacci had anarchist friends. He voluntarily produced his own .32 caliber Spanish automatic and said that Coacci had owned a Savage automatic. A year later Stewart wrote that he had discussed his suspicions of Coacci with police officers as early as 17 April, but he did not arrest Boda on 20 April. Curiously, evening papers for 20 April and morning papers for 21 April reported that a Quincy state senator had introduced a resolution in the legislature authorizing a fifteen-thousand-dollar reward for the capture of the perpetrators of the Braintree and Bridgewater holdups and another recent holdup of a bank in Randolph.[37] Stewart returned to Puffer's Place the next day but found no one at home. Two days later police officers found the home vacant. Stewart arranged with Simon Johnson, the owner of the garage where Boda's car was being repaired, to call him if Boda ever came for his car. He already suspected that Boda had hidden the Buick used in the South Braintree crime in his shack, although had he interrogated Boda's neighbors he would have learned that none of them had ever seen such a car in the shack.[38]

In the meantime, Boda's friend Bartolomeo Vanzetti was preoccupied with the arrest of Salsedo and Elia, of which he had been informed by friends in New York, and the interrogation of Felicani in Boston on 19 March. A 24 April anarchist meeting at the Italian Naturalization Club in East Boston detailed Vanzetti to travel to New York. He returned on 29 April without having learned a great deal more, but there could be no doubt that a new federal campaign against the Galleanisti had begun. Then, on the night of 2 May, Salsedo fell from a fourteen-story window in the New York building in which he and Elia were being held, and died. He was apparently a suicide; although his widow later sued the government for wrongful death, she did not claim that he had been murdered. The police and Salsedo's lawyer, Donato, both denied that he had been tortured.[39] What is certain—and what has been ignored by students of the case—is that on 4 May, both New York and Boston newspapers carried the story of Salsedo's death *and added that Salsedo had named the Galleani group of anarchists, headquartered in Lynn, Massachusetts, as having been responsible for the bombing outrages the previous year.*[40]

At their trial, Sacco and Vanzetti claimed that they went out on the next night—the night of 5 May—to collect incriminating anarchist literature and to store it in a safe place. This explanation probably approximates the truth. Now that they knew the government suspected their group of the 1919 bombings, they might logically have wanted to conceal *some* incriminating material and even, perhaps, an incriminating person such as Carlo Valdinocci. In any case, on the night of 5 May, Boda, Sacco, Vanzetti, and Ricardo Orciani came for the car, and Mrs. Johnson telephoned the police. Boda and Orciani departed on Orciani's motorcycle, but Sacco and Vanzetti were arrested in an electric car in Brockton shortly thereafter. Both men had weapons upon them. Sacco carried a loaded .32 Colt automatic and thirty-two cartridges, while Vanzetti had a loaded .38 Harrington and Richardson revolver. Orciani was arrested the next day; Boda hid out for several weeks before sailing to Italy.[41]

The arrest of Sacco and Vanzetti, then, resulted from a combination of two unrelated facts: Stewart's precipitous and almost completely unsupported conclusion that anarchists had perpetrated the Bridgewater and South Braintree holdups, and Salsedo's suicide, itself a result of the government's bombing investigations. The district attorney's office of Norfolk County, led by Frederick Katzmann, now assumed responsibility for the investigation of the two holdups.

Beginning on 6 May, numerous witnesses of both the Bridgewater and the South Braintree crimes came to Brockton to view the arrested men. Although, as we shall see, only a few of them tentatively identified them, Stewart and District Attorney Katzmann were certain they had found the "gang of anarchists" they had been seeking. The press headlined the arrests and noted Sacco and Vanzetti's anarchist connections. Within two days, huge headlines proclaimed that an assistant district attorney was "satisfied beyond any doubt" that *all three men* were involved in both crimes. Press reports substantially exaggerated the evidence against them.[42] An angry mob surrounded the courthouse in Brockton on 8 May when the three men were arraigned on minor charges, and a car carrying Orciani was mobbed in South Braintree when he was taken there to be viewed.[43]

Despite the headlines, however, the case against them was far from overwhelming. Although at least one witness identified Orciani as having been in South Braintree on 15 April, police on 12 May had to release him because the records at the foundry where he worked in Norwood showed he had been at work on that day. The suspects' fingerprints failed to match prints taken from the bandit car.[44] Captain William Proctor, the senior officer of the Massachusetts State Police who had been put in charge of the investigation of the South Braintree murders, did not believe that Sacco and Vanzetti had committed that crime.[45] To him it was the work of professional criminals. He did not think these anarchists capable of this carefully planned and cleverly executed robbery and murder.

Katzmann and Stewart, however, had committed themselves to their theory. They clung to it to their dying days, even believing that Orciani had managed to fake his time-clock alibi. In May preliminary hearings led to Vanzetti's being held for trial for the Bridgewater holdup attempt, while Sacco was held for the South Braintree murders. Vanzetti's trial was scheduled for June. It remained for the prosecution to develop evidence.

3 / *Vanzetti's Plymouth Trial*

anzetti's trial for the 24 December Bridgewater holdup was in many ways a dress rehearsal for the more important trial for the South Braintree murders. The prosecution's strategy was almost identical. Represented by J. P. Vahey and J. M. Graham, two well-known criminal lawyers, Vanzetti went to trial before Judge Thayer on 23 June 1920. Assistant District Attorney William Kane presented the case for the prosecution; Katzmann cross-examined the defense witnesses and made the closing argument. Evidence against Vanzetti included identifications by several eyewitnesses; a shotgun shell found upon him at the time of his arrest which, it was argued, matched one found at the scene of the crime; and some evidence of what Judge Thayer called "consciousness of guilt" at the time of his arrest. The prosecution contended that Boda, whom they had never been able to find, had also participated in the robbery. In reply the defense produced about a dozen witnesses, all Italians or Italian-Americans, who swore to having seen the fish peddler Vanzetti delivering eels in Plymouth on 24 December, a day on which Italians traditionally eat eels. To the surprise of courtroom observers, Vanzetti did not take the stand.[1] The jury found Vanzetti guilty of both assault with intent to murder and assault with intent to rob. Judge Thayer eventually sentenced him to twelve to fifteen years in prison.

Recent studies of the general reliability of eyewitness testimony have shown beyond any doubt that witnesses' recollections of events—and particularly of traumatic, stressful events—are highly unreliable, especially after the passage of weeks or months. Identifying previously unknown individuals is beyond the capability of most eyewitnesses. People have particular difficulty identifying people of a different race, and the ways in which many witnesses referred to Italians and other foreigners during testimony in the trials of Sacco and Vanzetti show clearly that Yankees regarded immigrants as members of different racial groups. Experiments have also shown that subjects respond readily to the suggestions of interrogators seeking to tailor their testimony to fit a predetermined theory.[2] The reports of a brief investigation of the Bridgewater holdup attempt undertaken by Pinkerton detectives in December 1919 and January 1920 show how these phenomena operated in this particular case.

At Vanzetti's trial in Plymouth in June 1920 the prosecution alleged that Vanzetti was the bandit who had stood in the street during the attempted holdup and fired a shotgun at the payroll truck. On the day of the crime a Pinkerton operative had interviewed the best witnesses to the holdup attempt. Earl Graves, the driver of the truck, described the shotgun bandit as five feet, six inches tall, weighing 145 pounds, thirty-five years old, of dark complexion, with a black mustache, and looking like a Greek. Graves identified the bandit car as a Hudson. Paymaster Alfred Cox described the bandit as "5'8", 150 lbs., dark complexion, 40 years of age. . . . He had a closely cropped mustache which might have been slightly grey." He did not identify the make of the auto. Benjamin Bowles, the third man in the truck, described him as "5'7", 35 or 36 years, 150 lbs., had a black closely cropped mustache, red cheeks, slim face, black hair and was an Italian or a Portugese [sic]." The driver he described as "light complexioned" and said that he wore a "black cap." He did not identify the car. Frank Harding, who worked in a garage and saw the holdup, said the man with the shotgun was "slim, 5' 10". . . . I did not get much of a look at his face but think he was a Pole." He identified the car precisely as "a black Hudson #6 auto" and gave the license number as 01173C. The descriptions of the bandit are fairly general, but the car seems definitely to have been a Hudson. Harding must have paid close attention to the car in order to get the license number, and garagemen can generally identify late-model cars at a glance.[3] The Pinkerton reports, which would have been crucial evidence at Vanzetti's trial, were unknown to the defense until 1926.

The Pinkertons learned that the license plate had been stolen from Hassam's garage, Needham, Massachusetts, sometime between 20 December and 24 December. They were briefly misled by a 26 December report that a black Buick seven-passenger touring car had been stolen from Needham on the evening of Sunday, 22 December. They soon learned that the car had actually been stolen on 22 *November*, but by then the theory that this was the bandit car had already taken hold. A Pinkerton operative apparently passed the report on to Chief Stewart on the evening of 26 December, and by 27 December two new witnesses to the Bridgewater crime had identified the bandit car as a Buick. On 29 December Chief Stewart and State Officer Brouillard said that they had concluded that the bandit car was a Buick and had "every reason to believe" that it was the car stolen from Needham.[4] Despite several promising leads, the Pinkerton investigation terminated abruptly in early January 1920 when the L. Q. White Company evidently decided not to spend any more money investigating a bungled robbery attempt.

On 17 April horseback riders discovered the bandit car used in South Braintree in the Manley Woods in Bridgewater. It was the Buick stolen on 22 November, and this persuaded Stewart that the same car and the same men had been involved in both robberies. After Sacco and Vanzetti were arrested they became suspects in both the Bridgewater and the South Braintree crimes. Although Vanzetti bore a general resemblance to the original descriptions of the shotgun bandit at Bridgewater, his appearance differed from the bandit's in one crucial way: his mustache was not "closely cropped," as described by Cox and Bowles, but long and flowing—and at the trial several witnesses, including a Plymouth policeman, testified that it always had been. Bowles, a special constable of the town of Bridgewater, saw Vanzetti at the Brockton police station on 6 May; Cox and Harding saw him on 7 May, *after* pictures of Sacco and Vanzetti had appeared in the Boston and local papers. Later that day a Pinkerton operative met them in Bridgewater and showed them more pictures of Sacco and Vanzetti. At that time Cox and Bowles "said Vanzetti bore a strong resemblance to one of the men in the party that attempted to steal the L. Q. White payroll last December, and probably is the man they saw." Incredibly, Harding, who said in December that he "did not get much of a look" at the shotgun bandit's face, now said "that Vanzetti is the man he saw, and that as soon as he saw Vanzetti in the Brockton Police station, he immediately recognized him as the man he saw in the party attempting to steal the L. Q. White payroll last December." (Harding in December *had* described the two other bandits in the street in more detail, but he had specified that both of them were clean-shaven.) Graves, the driver, could not testify; he had died in March.[5] Though inconsistent with earlier testimony, these identifications are not really surprising. It is almost impossible for a witness to retain a clear picture of a briefly glimpsed individual four and one-half months after the event. The witnesses' testimony probably reflected Stewart's certainty that he had gotten the bandits. Vanzetti's picture, which Bowles and Harding had probably seen before they saw the man himself, may also have helped secure these identifications.

Cox, Bowles, and Harding testified at a preliminary hearing in the Brockton Police Court on 18 May. Cox again declined to identify the make of the car and repeated that the shotgun bandit had "a short croppy mustache." Assistant District Attorney Kane asked Cox if he could identify any of the bandits.

A. I can identify the man with the shotgun.

Q. Where is he now? A. The man might look different today.

Q. Can you tell where that man is now? [Evidently the witness paused.]

THE COURT. Answer to the best of your knowledge and belief.

A. That's where it hinges on being positive.

MR. KANE. To the best of your knowledge and belief where is that man now? A. I think there is a doubt.

THE COURT. You can testify either positively or to the best of your knowledge and belief.

MR. KANE. To the best of your judgment do you know where that man is now? A. I feel—

THE COURT. Not what you feel. If you think you know the man say so. What judgment do you form to the best of your ability considering all the circumstances? A. How do you want it worded?

THE COURT. The say [sic] you remember it. A. I think it is this man behind the rail, the man with the moustache.

MR. KANE. To the best of your judgment and belief is that the man? A. I think he looks enough like the man to be the man.[6]

Bowles gave no opinion as to the make of the car. He also reaffirmed that the bandit had a "short croppy mustache," but he definitely identified Vanzetti as the shotgun bandit: "That is the man who had the shotgun that morning." He had also identified either Sacco or Orciani as the bandit in the street with a revolver, but both had good alibis for 24 December.[7]

The garageman Harding's testimony showed the most dramatic change. Having previously described the car as a #6 Hudson, he now identified it as a Buick. The shotgun bandit, whom in December he claimed to have hardly seen, suddenly became "a man of medium height, dark complected. . . . Hair cut close in back. Moustache, dark. . . . It seemed to be croppy. Not little and small, but one trimmed up. . . . High cheek bones. . . . Swarthy, dark complected." Harding said that there was "no question in my mind" that Vanzetti was he.[8]

At the trial, Cox gave a much more detailed description of the shotgun bandit: "That man was five feet eight, of slight build, that is, not a heavy man . . . of medium complexion, with prominent cheekbones, rather high; he had a short, well trimmed mustache. . . . The appearance of his forehead was long, that is, it had the appearance of a high forehead to me at the time, a long forehead. His hair was not especially thick. What there was of it as I could see him, stood up." Asked whether he had seen the man again, Cox replied, "I feel that I have," and indicated Vanzetti. Though confronted with his earlier testimony on cross-examination, he stuck to his story.[9]

Bowles, who had never before given any opinion as to the make of the bandit car, now described it as "a dark colored Buick car" and identified it as the auto found in Manley Woods. He gave essentially the same description of the shotgun bandit and said he was "positive" that it was Vanzetti. The mustache, which he had previously described as "closely cropped" and a "short croppy mustache," now became "very dark, trimmed at the ends" and "bushy," implying that a quick trim would have given Vanzetti's mustache the same appearance. Cross-examination revealed Bowles to be a constable of the town of Bridgewater, and he admitted having discussed the case with Chief Stewart. He also admitted that he had had no opinion of the make of the car on 24 December.[10]

When Harding took the stand, the black Hudson he had seen in December became "A large car, dark car either blue or black, I should say, a seven passenger Buick." His description of the bandit was expanded to include "a round head, bullet shaped, I should call it." He once again identified Vanzetti as the bandit. Vahey's cross-examination referred to the discrepancies in his description, especially with regard to the mustache.[11] Another witness, Georgina Brooks, identified Vanzetti as the man she saw *at the wheel* of the bandit car; this of course differed from all the other accounts, which distinguished the driver and the shotgun bandit, and conflicted with substantial evidence that Vanzetti never knew how to drive.[12] A fourteen-year-old boy, Maynard Shaw, also identified Vanzetti as a bandit he had seen firing a shotgun from about fifty yards away, stating that he could tell the man was a foreigner by the way he ran. Regarding the car, Shaw apparently began to say that he thought it was a Hudson but had later learned it was a Buick, but was cut off by Kane and said that it was either a Hudson, a Buick, or another type he could not remember. Two other witnesses, Richard Casey and John King, identified it as a Buick.[13]

Both the jury and, later, Governor Alvan Fuller, gave great weight to the eyewitness identifications of Vanzetti. Read against the background of the Pinkerton reports they lost most, if not all, of their credibility. The changes in the witnesses' descriptions do not necessarily reflect any particularly disreputable tactics on the part of the prosecution. It is not in the least unusual for witnesses to make false identifications, particularly after long lapses of time. Undoubtedly, after two chances to see Vanzetti personally, first at the police station on 7 May and then at the preliminary hearing—not to mention several opportunities to look at his picture—the image of Vanzetti's face impressed itself upon the witnesses' minds far more deeply than that of the bandit whom they had seen fleetingly, if at all, on 24 December. The changes in Bowles's and Harding's identifications of the car, however—particularly that of Harding, a garageman who initially gave a precise description of a #6 Hudson—suggest successful coaching by the prosecution. Worse, Chief Stewart's trial testimony indicates that he concealed documentary evidence of Harding's original identification. Stewart testified that Harding had given him an envelope on the day of the crime with the license number of the car on it, but the Bridgewater police chief now claimed to have lost it.[14] The inference that the envelope also had the words "#6 Hudson" on it is inescapable.

In assembling identification evidence the prosecution seems to have made do rather indiscriminately with whatever it could get, regardless of weaknesses in its witnesses' stories or contradictions with their initial statements. Equally significant is the prosecution's handling of the physical evidence against Vanzetti. The prosecution tried to link an exploded shotgun shell found at the scene of the crime immediately after the shooting to four shells found on Vanzetti at the time of his arrest. Dr. J. M. Murphy, a physician, found the shell and some shot on the street in Bridgewater. Although the Pinkerton reports of December and January 1919 do not mention the shell, Dr. Murphy on 10 May told Henry Hellyer, one of the Pinkertons, that he had found a twelve-gauge Winchester shell and some shot—"apparently" number 10 shot—in the road immediately after the attempted holdup. Hellyer's report indicates that Dr. Murphy had previously discussed his find with another Pinkerton operative. Three days earlier Hellyer had noted, "I turned the envelope containing shot over to Assistant District Attorney Kane," and while he did not specify what shot he meant, the shot found by Dr. Murphy seems to be the only possibility. On 11 May Hellyer noted that he had given the shotgun shell to Captain Proctor.[15] The prosecution, then, had the shell, the shot, and Dr. Murphy's story that the shot was number 10, a very small shot suitable for hunting birds but hardly likely to do any great bodily harm to a human being.

The shells introduced as having been found on Vanzetti, on the other hand, contained buckshot. In *The Case That Will Not Die*, Herbert Ehrmann raised serious questions as to whether the shells introduced at the Plymouth trial, and later in Dedham, actually were the ones taken from Vanzetti at the time of his arrest.[16] While Ehrmann's argument is speculative, the manner in which the prosecution used these shells to link Vanzetti to the crime and persuade the jury to return a verdict of assault with intent to murder is equally serious.

The prosecution faced two problems. Since the shells claimed to have been found upon Vanzetti contained buckshot, they could not be shown to connect him with the crime if Dr. Murphy's evidence that the shot he found was number 10 were admitted. Murphy's evidence would also militate against a guilty verdict on the charge of assault with intent to murder, since it would be difficult to argue that a bandit firing number 10 shot was firing with intent to kill. Thus the prosecution apparently induced Dr. Murphy to change his testimony. On direct examination he referred merely to finding a shell and identified the one in evidence as having been marked by him. Vahey's brief cross-examination was as follows:

> Q. Do you do any hunting, Doctor? A. I do.
> Q. It is the ordinary bird shell, is it not? A. No, I don't know what shot it is.
> Q. Such a shell as you use in hunting for birds, isn't it? A. Use it for anything.
> Q. Small birds? A. Sure.
> Q. Is it the ordinary gauge? A. Yes.[17]

Earlier Murphy had recalled finding number 10 shot, and the prosecution seems to have had the shot in its possession. It is difficult to believe that Kane did not induce him to give vaguer testimony. The state subsequently called Captain Proctor, qualified him as an expert, and induced him to say that the shell found on the street was "identical" to the loaded Winchester shell found on Vanzetti, "only that one is loaded and the other empty." The transcript does not include any comments on the weight of the shot.[18] By stressing the "identity" of the two Winchester shells the prosecution apparently wanted to convey to the jury both that Vanzetti's shells showed his participation in the robbery and that the shotgun bandit had used buckshot. They succeeded beyond their wildest dreams. After deliberating for several hours the jury returned to ask Judge Thayer for further instruction with respect to a possible verdict of assault with intent to murder. Thayer replied that such a verdict should be returned if the jury believed that the defendant had fired a weapon capable of causing death or great bodily harm. Returning to the jury room, the jurors attempted to answer this question *by opening the shells introduced as having been found on Vanzetti to see what kind of shot they contained.* Finding buckshot within, they apparently jumped to the utterly unfounded—and, as we know, wrong—conclusion that the shotgun bandit had been firing buckshot as well. They returned a verdict of guilty of assault with intent to murder. For the time being the prosecution's subterfuge had succeeded.[19]

Thayer and Katzmann both learned about the jury's tampering with the evidence immediately after the trial but did nothing about it. One juror later swore an affidavit that Katzmann had said that he "did not want it known." When Thayer sentenced Vanzetti in August—before the defense, which subsequently investigated the jury's tampering, knew what had occurred—he "placed on file" the conviction for assault with intent to murder, that is, he effectively nullified it and made any appeal of it impossible, while imposing an extraordinarily long sentence on Vanzetti for assault with intent to rob.[20]

The prosecution also tried to show consciousness of guilt on Vanzetti's part on the night of his arrest. Called to the stand, Chief Stewart produced notes of his interrogation of Vanzetti. Vanzetti had said he had been in Bridgewater to see a friend, Pappi; he had denied knowing Boda or Coacci; he had denied having seen a motorcycle that night; he had denied having been in Bridgewater before; and he had essentially admitted his anarchist beliefs while denying membership in any club or society. In a long discussion outside the presence of the jury Katzmann argued for admitting Vanzetti's denials with respect to knowing Boda or being in Bridgewater. Boda, he argued, was the driver of the bandit car and could be tied to the crime in several other ways as well.[21] This was critical to the whole prosecution theory of both crimes. At Dedham the prosecution suggested that Boda had kept the bandit car in his shed behind Puffer's Place and emphasized that it had been found in the Manley Woods only about a mile from his house.

Here in the Plymouth trial the prosecution had already produced a young man, Napoleon Joseph Enscher, who lived down the street from Puffer's Place. A potentially critical witness with respect to both crimes, he testified he had seen Boda driving a Buick "some time this spring." He lessened the value of his testimony extremely when Assistant District Attorney Kane asked him when this occurred. Testifying on 25 June, he replied, "Well, probably a month ago, four or five weeks ago, I should say—no [Did Kane blanch?], it was longer than that. I should say about seven or eight weeks ago. About eight weeks ago; it was the time when the roads were muddy." Eight weeks ago would have placed the date at 22 April, one full week after the South Braintree crime, but Vahey inexplicably failed to cross-examine.[22] Many neighbors had known Boda and Coacci, but Enscher was the only one to come forward with such testimony; we shall see that the others denied ever having seen Boda with a Buick.

Enscher's evidence would be competent only if the prosecution could place Boda among the bandits. The witness Richard Casey had described the driver as "shorter than the man that was sitting on his right. He had a kind of dark, soft hat and had a short moustache and he was of a rather swarthy complexion. . . . he had dark hair and he had a rather short, well trimmed moustache and a rather prominent nose."[23] Attempting to identify this man by implication, Chief Stewart described Boda as "five feet three inches, possibly five feet four inches high . . . with a long face, inclined to be long, swarthy, had a black moustache; it was a moustache that was trimmed up on his lip. . . . He had on a green velour hat the day I was talking to him."[24] Other witnesses described Boda as an inch or two shorter than this and added that he weighed only about 120–25 pounds.[25] Although Richard Casey's testimony was not much to go on, it established a link.

In an attempt to strengthen the link the prosecution called George H. Hassam of Hassam's garage, Needham, to testify as to the theft of the number plates used in the robbery and to describe the unknown man who had asked to borrow them. On direct examination he stated merely that he was "Italian"; on cross-examination he described him as "about five feet six or seven inches, dark hair and dark eyes, short croppy moustache, rather swarthy complexion." He said he wore a suit, no overcoat, and a cap. On 26 December he had described the man as "5'8", 165 lbs., stocky build, black hair, dark sallow complexion, black eyes, black mustache, clipped close; dressed in black lightweight overcoat, flannel shirt and black soft hat."[26] Once again a prosecution witness had changed his story to fit the prosecution's case; Hassam's original description could not possibly have applied to Boda.

The testimony of Simon Johnson and his wife established Vanzetti's presence in Bridgewater on the night of 5 May together with Sacco, Orciani, and Boda. His denial of acquaintance with Boda was accepted as legitimate evidence of consciousness of guilt, and Thayer apparently instructed the jury to take note of it, depending on their own interpretation of the testimony of these witnesses.[27] We shall see that the prosecution relied more heavily on consciousness of guilt at the Dedham trial.

Judge Thayer's conduct of the trial would strike almost any reader of the transcript as perfectly fair, and even Vanzetti, writing immediately after the trial, did not object to it. But Thayer's real feelings about Vanzetti surfaced when he passed sentence upon him in August. The sentence was not for assault with intent to murder—Thayer had effectively nullified that conviction—but for the less serious charge of assault with intent to rob. Just two months earlier Thayer had sentenced a man who pleaded guilty to assault with intent to murder to three years in the state House of Correction. Another man originally indicted on the same charge had pleaded guilty to assault with a dangerous weapon and been sentenced by Thayer to just six months in the same place. A few months later, in December 1920, a man pleaded guilty to armed robbery in Dedham court and received six to eight years. Judge Thayer sentenced Vanzetti to twelve to fifteen years in Charlestown State Prison—by far the longest sentence given any defendant in either Plymouth or Dedham for any noncapital crime over a three-year period from 1919 through 1921.[28]

Until Vanzetti's conviction at Plymouth the prosecution had hesitated to indict him for the South Braintree crime. Only one witness had placed him in South Braintree, one additional witness had placed him in the getaway car far south in Matfield, and the physical evidence against him amounted to one shotgun shell which, the prosecution had claimed at Plymouth, matched a shell found near the bandit car in the Manley Woods. But with the help of a new identification witness the prosecution decided to seek an indictment of Vanzetti for murder after his Plymouth conviction. The successful prosecution of Vanzetti for the lesser charge undoubtedly influenced their decision as well, just as their successful use of eyewitness testimony, physical evidence, and "consciousness of guilt" helped shape their strategy in the murder case.

3. Webster Thayer. (Courtesy Boston Public Library)

4 / The Prosecution

ad Vanzetti been acquitted in his Plymouth trial, it is quite likely that the murder charges against both him and Sacco would have been dropped. No indictments had yet been brought, and the evidence against the two men for the Braintree murder was not strong. After Vanzetti's conviction, however, the prosecution decided actively to pursue the case. Katzmann now took the murder investigation out of the hands of Captain Proctor and turned it over to Bridgewater Police Chief Michael Stewart. Proctor, the senior police officer in the Commonwealth, had far more experience than Stewart, but Stewart, unlike Proctor, believed in the case against Sacco and Vanzetti. Albert Brouillard, another state policeman, continued to assist Stewart.[1] The defense also made changes not long after. With the death penalty looming over the heads of the two men, Sacco and Vanzetti dropped the services of Vahey and Graham, who had represented them in the preliminary hearings and in Vanzetti's trial. Vanzetti now called upon his friend Carlo Tresca, an anarcho-syndicalist headquartered in New York, and Tresca secured the services of Fred Moore, a leading West Coast radical lawyer with some earlier Massachusetts experience, to take the defense.

On 9 and 10 September 1920 Frederick Katzmann asked a Dedham grand jury to indict Sacco and Vanzetti for murder. The proceedings illustrate the extraordinary latitude that prosecutors still enjoy before grand juries. Evidence against the men remained slim. At the preliminary hearing for Sacco on 26 May, three witnesses out of the more than thirty who saw some part of the South Braintree holdup had said that Sacco *resembled* one of the bandits they had seen: Lewis Wade, who referred to a man whom he had seen shoot Berardelli, and Mary Splaine and Frances Devlin, who said they had seen a man leaning out of the getaway car. None of them had positively identified him. Now, before the grand jury, Wade positively identified Sacco, and Katzmann badgered and cross-examined Splaine and Devlin until they stated with certainty that Sacco was the man they had seen.

Evidence against Vanzetti was much weaker; Katzmann could not call one witness who placed him at the scene of the crime. The only witnesses against him were John W. Faulkner, who claimed to have seen him alight from a train in East Braintree on the morning of 15 April, and

4. Frederick Katzmann. (Courtesy Boston Public Library)

Austin Reed, a gate tender in Matfield who had apparently seen the bandit car about an hour after the crime and identified Vanzetti as a man in the car who had shouted at him. The grand jurors had no way of knowing that at least thirty witnesses with an equally good or better opportunity to view the defendants had failed to identify either one. No physical evidence of any kind was introduced.[2]

The grand jury returned murder indictments for both men, but Katzmann could hardly have faced the prospect of a trial with any great confidence in the evidence he had. Perhaps for that reason, no trial date was set. The prosecution did nothing to gather new evidence against the two men, and the case disappeared from the newspapers. But in January 1921 it burst out on page 1 again in connection with an extraordinary episode—a purported offer from the prosecution to the defense committee to arrange a favorable disposition of the case relayed by a court interpreter, Angelina De Falco.

The significance of this episode must be understood within the specific context of the case. Accounts of the case of Sacco and Vanzetti have tended to leave a misleading image of the criminal justice system within which it was tried. Authors on all sides of the case have created an image of a stern Massachusetts judiciary and Southeastern District[3] prosecutor's office handing out harsh justice to criminals of all kinds. This view is romantic but inaccurate. A study of the disposition of all criminal indictments in Dedham and Plymouth superior courts for the years 1919, 1920, and 1921—a total of about four hundred criminal cases—gives an entirely different picture.[4] Far from applying a harsh and unbending law, these courts functioned similarly to criminal courts today. Minor offenses generally went unpunished, counsel frequently resolved even very serious cases by plea bargaining, and full-scale trials were quite rare. This is the background against which Mrs. De Falco's offer to fix the case for the defense must be analyzed.

Of the four hundred indictments returned in these courthouses in 1919–21, over three hundred related to minor offenses, especially breaking and entering and larceny. The vast majority of defendants to these charges pleaded guilty and were placed on probation. Prison capacity being far more limited in 1920 even than now, it was apparently impossible to sentence criminals to jail for such common crimes, except in cases of multiple offenses.

A more detailed analysis of sixty-seven more serious indictments, including eight for murder, four for manslaughter, eight for manslaughter involving an automobile, six for assault with intent to murder, three for assault with a dangerous weapon, eight for rape, nine for statutory rape, seven for assault with intent to rape, one for armed robbery, three for assault with intent to rob, and ten for miscellaneous crimes, shows considerable flexibility even in dealing with these serious crimes. Most of them were settled with a plea, many of the defendants were punished lightly or not at all, and even the most serious crimes were often settled by pleas to reduced charges.

Thus, of these sixty-seven serious crimes, only twenty-one went through a full trial. Thirteen of these twenty-one trials resulted in verdicts of guilty. In the remaining forty-six cases seventeen defendants entered initial pleas of guilty, nineteen changed not guilty pleas to guilty, and ten abandoned not guilty pleas and pleaded guilty to reduced charges. Plea bargaining, then, resolved more than two-thirds of all serious indictments. Sentencing statistics suggest that those defendants brave enough to insist upon a trial ran a considerable risk. About 40 percent of the defendants who eventually entered guilty pleas were sentenced to probation or a small fine: twelve out of the thirteen who were convicted after pleading not guilty received jail sentences. Over half of these defendants retained counsel.[5] Most popular counsel were J. J. McAnarney, who later represented Sacco and Vanzetti; Francis Squires, the clerk of the Dedham court; and Percy Katzmann, brother of Frederick Katzmann. Between them these three lawyers appeared for one-third of all defendants retaining counsel. They took an even higher proportion of the most serious crimes.

Sentencing practices do not seem very harsh even by contemporary standards. Thus, out of eight defendants convicted of rape, half served no prison sentence whatever, and two others served less than two years. Judge Thayer, who sat on Sacco and Vanzetti's cases, was especially lenient toward rape defendants. Not one of three persons convicted of assault with a dangerous weapon went to jail; two of three convicted of assault with intent to murder received sentences of between three and five years. Only one of three defendants indicted and convicted of manslaughter went to jail. And of eight murder defendants, one was found not guilty; two pleaded guilty to manslaughter and received sentences of less than two years; one, found guilty of manslaughter, received nine to twelve years (the most dramatic evidence of the risk of going through a trial); three were found guilty of second-degree murder and sentenced to life; and in one case, that of Sacco and Vanzetti, the defendants were convicted of first-degree murder and ultimately executed —the automatic penalty for first-degree murder at that time. It should be noted that the South Braintree killings seem to have been the most cold-blooded, premeditated murders to have come before the courts during this period.

This background suggests that the prosecution might have been willing to undertake some plea bargaining in the case of Sacco and Vanzetti. In late December 1920—three months after the grand jury indictments but before a trial date had been set—the Dedham Courthouse interpreter, Angelina De Falco, approached the Sacco and Vanzetti Defense Committee with a proposition. For fifty thousand dollars—later reduced to forty thousand, with the further concession that only five thousand need be paid at once—she offered to secure the two men's freedom. As she explained matters to Aldino Felicani and other defense committee members, they must discharge their present local counsel and retain Francis Squires and Percy Katzmann. Frederick Katzmann would withdraw from the case—he apparently never appeared when his brother represented the defendant—and the jury would be fixed with the cooperation of the district attorney's office. Mrs. De Falco said that *Vanzetti*, because of his prior conviction, would be the more difficult of the two to free. She also said that she had managed to help other defendants and apparently provided some examples. Felicani and many of the other anarchists wanted to pursue the matter, but Fred Moore, fearing a trap, refused to let them attend a meeting at Mrs. De Falco's house in Dedham where she had promised to introduce them to Francis Squires and Percy and Frederick Katzmann. Instead, the defense sent someone to check the license numbers of cars outside her home on the night of the meeting and subsequently discovered that they belonged to Squires and Percy Katzmann.[6]

Rather than respond to these overtures, Moore secured Mrs. De Falco's arrest on 15 January and arranged for her prosecution on a charge of soliciting legal business. Her trial during the last week in January was a sensation, both because of the implication of corruption in Norfolk County and because of the refusal of many of the witnesses from the defense committee to take the customary oath to tell the truth owing to their disbelief in God. Mrs. De Falco herself confirmed that she had spoken with defense committee members but claimed that they had initiated the contacts and added that they had admitted that the two men were guilty. Francis Squires said that he had never been interested in taking the case but confirmed that he had agreed to meet defense committee representatives at Mrs. De Falco's home. Frederick Katzmann claimed never to have heard of Mrs. De Falco. The judge, Michael

Murray, took a dim view of the proceedings from the start and ultimately found her innocent while publicly exonerating Frederick Katzmann, Percy Katzmann, and Francis Squires of any wrongdoing.[7] The episode undoubtedly did the defense no good whatever.

The question of whether Mrs. De Falco could actually have delivered what she promised is clearly of supreme importance. Was the prosecution capable of corruption of this kind? And why might they have been willing to drop all or part of their case against Sacco and Vanzetti? Such corruption *did* exist within the Massachusetts court system. In 1921 and 1922 the Supreme Judicial Court of the Commonwealth removed from office Nathan A. Tufts, district attorney of the Northern District (Cambridge and many cities and towns to the north and west), and Joseph C. Pelletier, district attorney of Suffolk County (Boston and surrounding towns). Between them they had taken bribes in return for favors at virtually every stage of the judicial process, accepting money in return for pledges not to seek indictments, to drop existing indictments, and to allow pleas to lesser charges and recommend light sentences. Both had also used threats of prosecution to extort money from various individuals and corporations.[8] Closer to home, Mrs. De Falco herself was convicted in 1931 of having bribed an officer of the State Corrections Commission on behalf of a woman seeking her husband's parole. Joseph Ross, another interpreter who worked during the Sacco and Vanzetti trial, later went to jail for trying to bribe a judge.[9]

But had such episodes taken place in the Southeastern District? Mrs. De Falco seems to have told the defense committee about several cases in which she had been of service to defendants, and two specific cases surfaced in the course of her trial. With respect to one, the "Caruso murder trial" in which the defendant had been convicted, she admitted acting as interpreter for Francis Squires but denied having told Mrs. Caruso that she could secure her husband's release from state prison for five hundred dollars. Mrs. Caruso testified in rebuttal that Mrs. De Falco had made such an offer, and since this is precisely the offense for which Mrs. De Falco eventually went to jail Mrs. Caruso was probably telling the truth.[10] More interesting was the case of Carmina Frucci. In July 1920 Mrs. Frucci, a recent immigrant, had shot her husband several times and killed him in a domestic quarrel. Appearing in court the next day represented by one Harry Goldkranz, she was arraigned for murder, but after she retained Percy Katzmann she was indicted for the lesser charge of manslaughter. Percy Katzmann confirmed that Mrs. De Falco was acting for him in this case.[11] Mrs. Frucci had every reason to be pleased with the reduction of her charge. Defendants who killed their spouses more frequently stood trial for murder. The evidence of other cases suggests that Mrs. Frucci might have expected to be let off with a sentence of a few years had she pleaded guilty. Unfortunately for her, her case had not come to trial at the time of Mrs. De Falco's trial. Any chance of a plea bargain on the manslaughter charge apparently vanished after her case was mentioned in those well-publicized proceedings. At her trial three months later in April 1921 Mrs. Frucci pleaded not guilty, was convicted, and was sentenced to eight years in prison, definitely a harsh sentence by the standards then prevailing. Her case still suggests, however, that Mrs. De Falco and Percy Katzmann could arrange advantageous plea bargains for defendants in capital cases. Several other defendants apparently told the defense that Mrs. De Falco had tried to steer them to Percy Katzmann or Francis Squires.[12]

A few other Southeastern District cases also present suspicious features. The first, already discussed, is that of Sergis Zakoff, acquitted in April 1920 of advocating anarchy. Zakoff had retained Percy Katzmann, and the verdict of not guilty was both against the weight of the evidence and, evidently, not in conformity with Judge Thayer's charge. The jury may merely have balked at convicting a man for his opinions, but if any case during these years is open to a suspicion of jury tampering, this is certainly the one. The other case, about which much less is known, involved an Italian-American war veteran, Giacomo Ferrara of Hingham. Arrested and arraigned for shooting two men in the head and killing them in January 1921, he was eventually allowed to plead guilty to manslaughter and sentenced to just one year in jail. Research has unfortunately failed to turn up any more information about this case. Finally, in early 1922 a woman named Josie May Henry, whom the Sacco and Vanzetti defense had contacted regarding the activities of her husband, William Dodson, told a very similar story of courthouse corruption involving Percy Katzmann and Francis Squires.[13]

With respect to Sacco and Vanzetti, while it is doubtful that Mrs. De Falco could have made good on all her grandiose promises, her offer suggests a good possibility of disposing of the case without a trial. It seems very unlikely that she could actually have arranged to bribe the foreman of the jury in what was clearly going to be a highly publicized criminal case, but she may well have been in a position to arrange some kind of a deal, steering the defendants to Squires and Katzmann by assuring them that the district attorney's brother and the clerk of the Dedham court stood a good chance of arranging a favorable disposition of their cases.

The critical question is whether she actually had some indication from Squires, Percy Katzmann, or the prosecution that some kind of plea bargain was possible.

While the full facts of the episode will never be known, the Commonwealth in late 1920 was showing no eagerness to bring the case to trial. The grand jury minutes and the voluminous state police files released in 1977 show that its case was weak indeed. Only one witness had definitely identified Sacco at the scene of the crime, and only one other had definitely identified Vanzetti. Virtually no new evidence of any kind had been uncovered since their arrest in May. The prosecution seems to have had no theory tying either of the guns found upon the two men to the crime. A police spy who had been planted next to Sacco's Dedham jail cell had also failed to develop any new information.[14] Another police informer who contacted Katzmann about the case, one John Ruzzamenti, later swore an affidavit that Katzmann on 30 December 1920 had told him that he had "no evidence" against either man.[15] Public interest in the case had died down temporarily, and the district attorney's office might have been willing to reduce charges against one or both men rather than go to trial without more evidence. Although Francis Squires claimed on the stand that he had never wanted to take the case, he admitted that he had agreed to meet defense committee members at Mrs. De Falco's house.[16]

Had the defense committee attended the meeting, the conversation might quite possibly have turned to the chances of securing reduced charges for one or both defendants. Moore's decision to go public put an abrupt end to any such possibility. The prosecution began searching for new evidence immediately after Mrs. De Falco's arrest, and on 5 February the trial was set for 7 March. Three weeks later the defense moved for a continuance, and the trial was rescheduled for 31 May. In the meantime, the prosecution had begun developing evidence in earnest.

5 / The Identification Testimony

Beginning in January 1921, Stewart, Katzmann, and Assistant District Attorney Harold Williams developed the evidence that they ultimately presented at the Dedham trial. At that trial, which lasted from 31 May to 14 July 1921, the defense was conducted by Fred Moore and two local lawyers, J. J. McAnarney and William Callahan. Assistant District Attorney Williams presented the prosecution's case; Fred Katzmann cross-examined the defense witnesses and made the prosecution's closing argument.

As in Vanzetti's Plymouth trial, the prosecution relied on three kinds of evidence. First, eleven eyewitnesses identified Sacco and Vanzetti as having participated in various stages of the crime. Second, Katzmann argued strongly that Sacco and Vanzetti's behavior on the night of their arrest, and certain falsehoods he claimed they had told him on the day after their arrest, showed consciousness of guilt. Last, with respect to physical evidence, the prosecution claimed that Sacco's Colt had fired one of the bullets taken from Berardelli's body and one of four shells found near the scene of the crime, and that the Harrington and Richardson revolver found on Vanzetti at the time of his arrest had been taken from Berardelli during the robbery. We shall begin with the identification testimony, which consumed by far the most time at the trial.

With the exception of Robert Montgomery, whose book *Sacco-Vanzetti: The Murder and the Myth* essentially endorsed the prosecution case from top to bottom, previous works on the case have not been especially impressed by the eyewitness evidence against the two men. Many discrepancies in the witnesses' stories emerged during cross-examination, and others became clear when the reports of the Pinkerton investigation were discovered in 1926.[1] Although on the whole eyewitness testimony is too fallible to form the basis for a firm conclusion as to the guilt or innocence of the defendants, an examination of it does reveal a great deal about the way in which the prosecution prepared its case. Previously unavailable prosecution documents also shed new light upon the development of much of the eyewitness testimony. Viewed in light of their original statements, virtually none of the eleven prosecution witnesses emerges as a credible witness.

The South Braintree crime was well observed. The shooting of Parmenter and Berardelli took place in broad daylight, and dozens of people

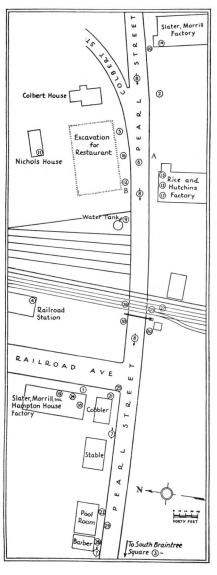

BEFORE THE SHOOTING

1. Neal
2. Andrews, Campbell
3. Tracy
4. Heron
5. Foley
6. Frantello
7. Novelli
8. Behrsin

DURING THE SHOOTING

9. Bostock
10. Wade
11. Nichols
12. McGlone
13. Langlois
14. Carter
15. Pelser
16. Laborers at excavation
17. Liscomb
 A. Where Berardelli fell
 B. Where Parmenter fell

AFTER THE SHOOTING

18. Splaine, Devlin
19. Carrigan
20. Levangie
21. DeBeradinis
22. Goodridge
23. Burke
24. Pierce, Ferguson
25. Cellucci
26. O'Neil
27. Workers on railroad
28. Damato
29. Olsen
30. Gould

5. The neighborhood of the crime. (Adapted, by permission, from Osmond K. Fraenkel, *The Sacco-Vanzetti Case* [New York: Knopf, 1931]. © 1931 by Alfred A. Knopf, Inc.; © 1959 by Osmond K. Fraenkel)

6. The path of the bandit car into South Braintree. The gate tender's shack is at the left; Slater and Morrill offices at right. (Courtesy Massachusetts Supreme Judicial Court)

either saw the shooting itself, witnessed the bandit car on its escape from South Braintree, or noticed the bandits in South Braintree earlier on the day of the crime. At the trial seven witnesses identified Sacco as a man they had seen in South Braintree before, during, or after the shooting. Not one witness to the shooting identified Vanzetti, but two placed him in the getaway car, one placed him in a car in South Braintree on the morning of the shooting, and one claimed to have seen him on a train from Cohasset to East Braintree that morning. These eleven obviously represented a small minority of the total number of witnesses to the shooting and its aftermath.

The first trial witness to identify Sacco was Mary Splaine, a bookkeeper in the offices of Slater and Morrill. From her office on the first floor of the firm, at the intersection of Pearl Street and the railroad tracks, she had seen the bandit car after it crossed the tracks. On 19 April she told a Pinkerton operative that she had seen a man "clad in light gray clothes leaning over the driver's seat from the rear," firing a revolver. "She described the man as follows from the momentary glimpse she got of him:—round, rather full pale face, black hair, cut pompadour style, powerful square shoulders and wearing gray clothes,

7. The Slater and Morrill factory. This picture was taken from the north side of Pearl Street, looking east. The bandit car waited in front of the factory, and Lewis Wade watched the shooting from in front of the small shack by the front steps. (Courtesy Massachusetts Supreme Judicial Court)

no hat." On 20 April she identified a photograph of Anthony Palmisano, a known criminal from New York State: "She described the man yesterday when I interviewed her and on seeing the photo today instantly declared that it was a photo of the man she saw standing in the car with a revolver in his hand and who wore light gray clothes." Three days later in Captain Proctor's Boston office she again "identified the photo of Anthony Palmisano as a photo of the man she saw standing in the bandits' auto holding a revolver as the car came up Pearl Street."[2] Other witnesses also identified Palmisano, but the Buffalo, New York, resident had to be eliminated as a suspect when inquiries revealed that he had been in jail on the day of the robbery.[3]

On 6 May, after Sacco and Vanzetti had been arrested, numerous witnesses came to the Brockton police station to look at them. Of fifteen witnesses who viewed Sacco, one, Lewis Wade, picked Sacco as the man he had seen shoot Berardelli, while several others, including Mary Splaine, said he bore some resemblance to a man they had seen.[4] On 7 May a Pinkerton operative showed photos of Sacco and Vanzetti to

8. The view from the second-floor window of the Slater and Morrill offices from which Mary Splaine and Francis Devlin saw the bandit car on Pearl Street (*left foreground*). Note their severely limited view of the street. (Courtesy Harvard Law School Library)

Mary Splaine, who had already seen the two men the day before. She now indicated that Sacco "looked like" the man she had seen leaning out of the window.[5]

On 26 May Mary Splaine was a witness at the preliminary hearing in Quincy District Court. "As the machine traveled half the distance between the railroad track and the sidewalk next to the office building," she testified, "I saw this man leaning towards the right of the machine, with one hand on the front seat as if to go over from the back into the front. He stood with one hand resting on the front seat and the other discharging."

Q. Have you seen this defendant [Sacco] before? A. Yes.
Q. Where? A. I am almost sure I saw him at Braintree, but I saw him at the Brockton police station afterwards.

On cross-examination she was less certain.

Q. Your opinion is he bears a striking resemblance to him? A. I could be mistaken.
Q. You are not sure he is the man? A. No.

. . . . . .

Q. Do you say this is the man? A. I will not swear positively he is
the man.

. . . . . .

Q. You did not get a sufficient look to say positively this is the
man? A. I would not swear positively he is the man.
Q. You don't feel certain enough of your own position to say he is
the man? A. I don't think my opportunity afforded me the right
to say he is the man.[6]

Four months later Katzmann called Mary Splaine as a witness before
the grand jury. He immediately confronted her with her previous vacil-
lations: "I am determined," he said, "that you shall answer the question
directly and that is something you never have done with me before."
Again and again, in response to repeated questioning, she repeated that
she *thought* Sacco was the man she had seen, adding that she could be
mistaken. Katzmann suggested that if Sacco had merely been playing
marbles, or if he were accused of committing a traffic violation, she
would say that he was the man. When she agreed he asked, "Are you not
a little bit cowardly?" After ten minutes of alternately badgering her
and disclaiming any desire to influence her, Katzmann got her to say
that when she first saw Sacco, "the minute I looked at him my impression was 'that's the man' "—not, in fact, what she had said at the
Brockton police station. "You have not any doubt he is the man?" he
concluded. "No Sir," she said.[7]

Nine months later at the Dedham trial she gave much more elaborate
and definite testimony. She denied that the man had been shooting
a gun or even that she had seen his right hand. "He was a man that I
should say was slightly taller than I am," she said, a rather extraordinary
statement, one should think, to make about an individual one had seen
inside an automobile. "He weighed possibly from 140 to 145 pounds. I
noticed particularly the left hand was a good sized hand, a hand that de-
noted strength. . . . the face was what we would call clear-cut, clean-cut
face. . . . The forehead was high. The hair was brushed back and it was
between, I should think, two inches and two and one-half inches in
length and had dark eyebrows." She said that Sacco was the man. Confronted on cross-examination with her previous testimony, she said on
redirect that further reflection after seeing Sacco in Quincy court had
led her to be certain.[8]

The Pinkerton reports also include evidence as to Miss Splaine's general reliability. On 20 April she had told one of the operatives that she suspected an office worker, one Lewis Darling, of having engineered the robbery, which had left him in line for Parmenter's job. Darling, she said, needed money to finance his stock speculations and expensive habits. Other office workers apparently shared this view. After sitting on this story for several weeks the Pinkerton operative finally decided to check it further on 11 May.

> As opportunities occurred, I made discreet inquiries about Mr. Darling, whom Miss Mary Splaine accused of being implicated in the murders and robbery. My inquiries show that there is absolutely no grounds for Miss Splaine's accusation, and that Mr. Darling enjoys Mr. Slater's confidence. Today I took the matter up with Mr. Frayer [Thomas Fraher, the Slater and Morrill superintendent]. He ridiculed the idea of Darling being implicated and further stated that no serious attention can be paid to Mary Splaine's stories, because she is one of the most irresponsible persons he ever came in contact with.[9]

Frances Devlin worked in the Slater and Morrill office with Mary Splaine and had seen the bandit car. Unfortunately, she did not discuss the case with the Pinkerton investigators, but she said upon viewing Sacco on 6 May that he "looks very much like" a man she had seen.[10] At the preliminary hearing she, too, had described a man leaning out of the car as it went over the crossing and shooting at the crowd. Asked, "Do you say positively that he is the man?" she had replied, "I don't say positively." Sacco, she said, "looks very much like the man that stood up in the back seat shooting."[11] At the grand jury she initially told Katzmann, "I will say that I think he is the man," and indicated that she was not sure she had had a good enough view, but after he questioned her further she allowed as how she was "sure."[12] At Dedham she testified that she was "sure" Sacco was the man and denied she had ever doubted it.[13] District Attorney Katzmann may perhaps be pardoned for his characterization of Splaine and Devlin in his closing argument:

> Gentleman, do you think that these two young women, presumably endowed with Christian instincts, young ladies who could have no enmity against the defendant Sacco, who could have no reason for committing the most damnable of perjuries

would bespeak evidence against a human being that would take his life away? Gentlemen, that passes the bounds of human credulity. You can't believe that. You cannot have looked on Mary Splaine, a smart business woman, you cannot have looked on the gentle Frances Devlin and have seen the truth shining like stars out of her young womanly eyes and believe for a moment that either or both of them would dare, before a court of justice or before God their Maker, condemn Sacco to his death with a wilful lie. You cannot believe that, gentlemen, having seen those women.[14]

Next to produce a positive identification was Lewis Pelser, a shoe cutter in the Rice and Hutchins factory facing the street where the shooting had taken place. Pelser admitted at the trial that he had told police officers in May of 1920 that he had not seen enough to identify anyone. On 26 March 1921 he had told a defense investigator named Robert Reid that he had looked out a slightly opened window, seen Berardelli lying on the ground, and ducked under the bench in fright without seeing any of the bandits. He did say that he had seen the license number on the bandit car—"49853, something like that"—but said he could not remember it exactly. This tallied perfectly with statements he had earlier given to State Police Officer Brouillard in late January 1921. Brouillard's notes indicate that Pelser had seen only the car and state specifically that he could not identify anyone.[15]

At the trial Pelser changed his story completely, stating that he had opened the window at once and seen a bandit fire one shot into Berardelli, who was already lying on the ground, and afterward fire across the street at Parmenter. (Later we shall see that this does not tally with the evidence of other eyewitnesses and with firearms and autopsy evidence.) Asked whether the man he saw shooting was in the courtroom he pointed to Sacco and said, "Well, I wouldn't say it was him, but he is a dead image of him." He also gave the license number as 49783. On cross-examination he said he had lied to Reid because he did not want to have to go to court.[16]

The defense later called William Brenner, Peter McCullum, and Dominic Constantino, all of whom had been working in the same room as Pelser and all of whom testified that Pelser had not been at the window during the shooting. Constantino more particularly said that all four of them, including Pelser, had ducked under a bench when they realized what was happening and that Pelser had subsequently remarked that he had got the number plate but had not seen anything. Constantino had contacted the defense committee after reading about Pelser's testimony in the newspaper.[17] After the trial Pelser signed contradictory affidavits for the defense and the state, first repudiating and then reaffirming his testimony.[18]

The next identifier of Sacco was Lola Andrews, who had gone to South Braintree with a friend, Julia Campbell, looking for work on the day of the murder. On 14 January 1920, Moore had questioned her at her home. She had told him that on her way into Slater and Morrill she had seen a light-complexioned man sitting in the back of the car and another man standing behind it. Coming out, she said, she had asked the man inside the car for directions to Rice and Hutchins. She told Moore she had seen newspaper pictures of the men arrested for the crime but had not recognized them, and she failed to identify further pictures of Sacco and Vanzetti that Moore showed her. At Dedham she said that a *dark* man had been working under the car when she came *out of Slater and Morrill*, that he had worn dark clothing, that she had asked *him* directions, that he had given them—and that he was Sacco. She admitted she had been to Dedham jail to see him since her talk with Moore.[19]

Other evidence confirms that Lola Andrews had changed her story not long before the trial. A Quincy police officer testified for the defense that Mrs. Andrews had told him in February that she had not seen the faces of the men she saw in South Braintree. She added that she had recently been to Dedham jail. A newspaper reporter corroborated this account. A Quincy tailor said that she had complained to him that the government had been pressuring her to make an identification; Judge Thayer, in perhaps his most prejudicial intervention in the trial, asked the man whether he had tried to find the government official who had pressured her.[20] The *Boston Globe* of 16 February 1921 reported that Lola Andrews had told the police that she had been assaulted in a corridor of the building in which she lived. She added that she had been in Dedham the day before, answering questions from the district attorney's office, and that "she had been pestered for weeks by people presenting both sides of the case who were trying to get her to talk."[21]

A summary of the shooting and of the identification testimony available to the prosecution, dictated by Katzmann on 23 February 1921, confirms that Lola Andrews had not identified Sacco at that time. Katzmann's summary refers to identifications by various witnesses, including Splaine, Devlin, Lewis Wade, Michael Levangie, and Carlos Goodridge, and it also refers to Lola Andrews's asking a man standing by the murder car how to get to Rice and Hutchins—but *it makes no mention of any identification of Sacco by Lola Andrews* and does not mention Pelser.[22] Between February and June something induced Andrews to change her mind.

Even more devastating was the testimony of Lola Andrews's companion Julia Campbell, whom the prosecution failed to produce and who they had implied could not see. When called by the defense she said they had seen a man under the car and a man by the fence wearing khaki clothes whom Lola Andrews had asked for directions to *Slater and Morrill.* They had gotten directions for Rice and Hutchins inside Slater and Morrill and had not spoken to either man on the way out. Julia Campbell's eyesight was poor, but she was hardly blind.[23] After the trial Moore discovered that Lola Andrews had an unsavory past, including experience in the world's oldest profession. Like Pelser, she first gave Moore an affidavit repudiating her testimony, then in turn repudiated that affidavit for Katzmann.[24]

Carlos E. Goodridge, who described himself as a salesman, had been playing pool on Pearl Street on the far side of the railroad tracks from the factories when the shooting took place. He had seen a man leaning out of the bandit car as it passed, and he identified the man as Sacco. He claimed to have viewed Sacco for the first time at Sacco's arraignment in September of 1920. Not until November 1920 had he discussed the case with any government official. Katzmann's 23 February memorandum stated that "Goodridge, with a fair degree of positiveness, is of the opinion that Sacco is the man" he had seen leaning out; at the trial Goodridge simply said that Sacco was the man. On cross-examination McAnarney attempted to show that Goodridge had charges pending against him in Norfolk County, but Thayer refused to allow this, claiming that only evidence of a conviction would be admissible.[25] As a matter of fact, Goodridge had pleaded guilty to larceny in Norfolk Superior Court on 28 September 1920 and was on probation when he testified.[26] It was at his own appearance for larceny that he had seen Sacco. The owner of the pool room, Peter Magazu, testified that Goodridge had described the bandit pointing the gun as a "young man with light hair, light complexion and [wearing] an army shirt." A barber, Nicola Damato, testified that Goodridge had denied seeing anyone. Another barber, Harry Arrogni, reported Goodridge as having said that he could not identify the man he had seen. Goodridge's employer, Andrew Manganio, testified that he had encouraged Goodridge to view Sacco and Vanzetti after their arrest; Goodridge had replied that he could not possibly remember the faces of the men he had seen.[27]

Goodridge's memory seems to have improved in the courtroom after he himself had been arrested. In statements to prosecution officials in February 1921 he not only identified Sacco but stated that he had seen Sacco and spoken to him about a week earlier at South Braintree station —a story the prosecutors apparently discouraged him from repeating on the stand.[28] After the trial Moore discovered that Goodridge was really Erastus Corning Whitney of upper New York State, an arsonist, forger, and bigamist.[29]

Two other witnesses placed Sacco in South Braintree before the shooting. William S. Tracy, a South Braintree real estate man, had seen two men standing in front of a drugstore at Hancock and Washington streets at about 11:40 on the day of the shooting. As he told Stewart and Brouillard on 15 February 1921, he had paid particular attention to the men because he owned the building in question and disliked having people lean against it. On that day—fully ten months after the crime— he said he was "sure" that the pictures he had subsequently seen of the two men in the newspapers were the men he had seen, but when he actually saw Sacco he would "not say positively that Sacco is one of the men he saw; he will say that Sacco resembles one of them very much; says he is the same build, color and height as the man he saw."[30] At the trial he went somewhat further. Asked whether Sacco was one of the men he saw, he used perfect legal phraseology: "While I wouldn't be positive, I would say to the best of my recollection that was the man." He admitted having seen pictures of the defendants.[31]

William J. Heron, a railway policeman, claimed to have seen two men in the train station at about 12:30 on 15 April. He now said Sacco was one of the men and that he had recognized him at Quincy Courthouse about six weeks after the crime—long after his picture had been published in the papers. He admitted on cross-examination that he had not taken much notice of the two men and that he had refused to talk to a defense investigator. New evidence shows that Heron had also been induced to alter his testimony to make it more plausible. Notes by Williams written in February or March of 1921 report that Heron "saw two men sitting near toilet door smoking" and that he was positive Sacco was one of them. Williams quickly added, in parentheses, that Sacco did not smoke.[32] Williams and Heron took care of this point nicely during Heron's trial testimony.

> Q. Will you describe the men you saw sitting there, and tell the jury what they were doing? A. One of them was about 5 feet 6 inches, weighed about 145 pounds, Italian. The other was about 5 feet 11; I should say, weighed about 160. They were smoking cigarettes, one of them.
> Q. Do you know which one was smoking? A. The tallest one.[33]

Only these witnesses provided identifications of Sacco. The trial testimony of Lewis Wade, whom the prosecution had pegged as its star witness, gave Williams an unpleasant shock. A shoemaker at Slater and Morrill, Wade was one of the eyewitnesses closest to the shooting. At the inquest on 15 April he described three bandits fairly comprehensively but expressed doubt as to whether he could identify them. He described the man who shot Berardelli as between nineteen and twenty-two years of age and "weighing 125 to 130 lbs. at most."[34] On 22 April he said that a picture of Anthony Palmisano "bore a great resemblance" to the man who shot Berardelli. Wade told his story to Captain Proctor the next day, but as a Pinkerton operative noted, "as he went along, it was evident that he did not have the remotest idea as to what the bandits actually looked like. He insisted that two of them were tall, heavily built men and that the third man and fourth man he saw were tall and slim. Capt. Proctor discarded Wade's testimony altogether.[35]

Stewart and Katzmann did not share Proctor's skepticism, and after Wade saw Sacco at the Brockton police station and identified him as the man he saw shoot Berardelli the prosecution marked him down as a star witness.[36] They stuck to these plans even after Wade refused to identify Sacco definitely at the Quincy preliminary hearing. At the grand jury proceedings Wade apologized for his testimony at the preliminary hearing and identified Sacco,[37] but at the trial he once again repudiated his identification—to the obvious consternation of Assistant District Attorney Williams—and said merely that Sacco resembled the man he saw.[38] Wade was immediately discharged by Slater and Morrill. The identification evidence against Sacco rested upon seven witnesses.

The prosecution must have known from the beginning that their eyewitness case against Vanzetti would be much weaker. Of fourteen eyewitnesses to the crime who viewed Vanzetti at Brockton on 6 May, thirteen stated categorically that they had never seen him before in their lives.[39] The exception was Michael Levangie, the gate tender at the Pearl Street railroad crossing. At the inquest on 17 April he said he had been lowering the gate for an oncoming freight train when the bandit car approached but raised it when he saw a gun pointing at him from the car. He described the driver, the only bandit he saw, as having a "dark complexion, dark brown mustache," and wearing a "soft hat and brown coat."[40] A Pinkerton investigator spoke to him the next day.

> Next I called on Michael Levangie, the crossing gate tender who saw the auto dash by. He related the following but it is doubtful if his story is of any value. First heard shots while cleaning the windows of his shanty. . . . A few minutes [later] a large black touring car with side curtains on came up the street at high speed driven by a man who Levangie describes as follows: 48–50 years, 160 lbs, stocky build, black hair, dark complexion, *clean shaven* [emphasis added] and long hooked nose, wearing brown Army coat and brown soft hat.[41]

The Pinkerton operative discounted the story because many other witnesses unanimously described the driver as blond and light-complexioned. But on 6 May Levangie was the only witness to identify Vanzetti as a South Braintree bandit; Vanzetti, he said, was the driver. The next day the Pinkerton investigator noted that this was a doubtful identification and reiterated that none of the other witnesses had placed Vanzetti in the murder party.[42]

Katzmann did not call Levangie before the grand jury, but the gate tender repeated his story at the trial, identifying Vanzetti as the driver of the car. A nervous and unconvincing witness, he claimed not to remember a conversation with McAnarney only two weeks earlier.[43] Edward Carter, a Slater and Morrill employee, later testified that Levangie had told him that the driver was "a light-complected man," and Henry McCarthy, a railroad fireman who had come through South Braintree just half an hour after the crime, testified that Levangie had said he would not be able to identify anyone whom he had seen.[44] In his closing argument Katzmann repudiated Levangie's identification of Vanzetti as the driver but hypothesized that Vanzetti had been sitting behind the driver instead.[45]

Despite Vanzetti's distinctive appearance, the prosecution had found only two more identification witnesses by the time of the trial. The first, John W. Faulkner, told one of the two most fantastic stories heard during the proceedings. On 15 April, he said, he had boarded the train from Cohasset to Boston—a train he took every day at that time. At the next several stations another passenger had asked whether that station was East Braintree, eventually alighting there. That man, he said, was Vanzetti. On cross-examination he admitted he could not describe another man who had relayed this passenger's question. He also said that although he had recognized pictures of Vanzetti in the newspapers he had not mentioned his story *to anyone* until July 1920, when he talked to the police. (Vanzetti's Plymouth trial had taken place during June of 1920, a fact the defense did not, of course, wish to bring out.)[46]

The defense called the conductor on the train, who produced documentary proof that no cash fares had been purchased between any of the stations around Plymouth and Braintree or East Braintree on that train on 15 April, and three ticket agents from the Plymouth area, whose records showed that no such ticket had been sold at their stations on 15 April and who did not recognize Vanzetti as having been in their station.[47] Faulkner's trial testimony was also at odds with his testimony before the grand jury; there he said that the man he saw on the train had "a short, stubby mustache." He also said that when he had seen Vanzetti at the Plymouth jail he had had no mustache at all![48]

Another gate tender, Austin Reed, had seen the bandit car at Matfield crossing at about 4:15—the latest sighting of the bandit car reported that day. He had lowered the gate when the car was approaching, and a man sitting on the driver's right had yelled, "What the hell are you holding us up for?" "What the hell did you hold us up for?" he repeated, when the car finally passed by. That man, he said, was Vanzetti. On cross-examination Reed vitally impeached the worth of his identification by stating that the bandit's English was "unmistakable and clear"; Vanzetti spoke with a very heavy accent. He added that he had gone to the Brockton police station on his own initiative several days after the arrest, and while confirming that pictures of the two defendants had already been published in the newspapers, he quickly denied having seen any before he went.[49]

At the outset of the trial the prosecution had just these three identification witnesses against Vanzetti, but a potential juryman, Harry Dolbeare of South Braintree, then stepped forward. On the morning of the murder he had seen a car in South Braintree Square with five men in it. He claimed to have recognized Vanzetti as one of the men in the car when called for jury duty, fully thirteen months after the crime. On cross-examination he said he could not describe any of the other men.[50] It is difficult to believe that he could have retained such a definite memory over a thirteen-month span of time. On 8 June, after Dolbeare had come forward but before he testified, he submitted to a long interview with Moore, during which he stuck to his story. After the interview was over, according to defense investigator Reid, Dolbeare "explained that he only got into this case as a reason for his escaping serving as a juryman."[51]

These eleven witnesses represented but a small minority of eyewitnesses to the shooting and the bandits' escape. Thirty-four other witnesses had seen one or more of the bandits and failed to identify either Sacco or Vanzetti. They include witnesses who testified at the inquest or spoke to the Pinkertons and who were therefore known to the prosecution but not the defense; witnesses interviewed by the police who did not testify; witnesses who testified at the trial; and one or two witnesses discovered by the defense after the trial. They may most usefully be broken down and measured against the prosecution witnesses according to the time at which they saw the bandits.

To begin with, six other witnesses saw one or more of the bandits in or around South Braintree on the day of the shooting—witnesses corresponding, that is, to Lola Andrews, Tracy, and Heron, who identified Sacco in various places, and Dolbeare, who claimed to have seen Vanzetti in the bandit car. Albert Frantello, a Slater and Morrill employee, had walked up to Pearl Street just before the murders. On 20 April 1920 he told a Pinkerton man he had seen two men loitering on the street and that he had seen one of them clearly. He gave a description of a shorter and slimmer man than either defendant and, shown the Palmisano photograph, "admitted his belief that it was a photo of the man he saw." Later he confirmed this identification to Captain Proctor. He stated at the trial that neither Sacco nor Vanzetti was one of the men he had seen. Jenny Novelli, a nurse, had seen the bandit car before the shooting and told a Pinkerton detective on 17 April that she had taken particular notice of one occupant because of a resemblance to an acquaintance of hers. At the trial she said neither of the men in the dock was in the automobile. Minnie Kennedy and Louise Hayes told the Pinkertons they had had the bandit car in sight for perhaps twenty minutes before the shooting; they had a good idea of the driver's appearance and never identified either Sacco or Vanzetti.[52] Ralph DeForrest, an unemployed shoemaker, testified at the inquest to having seen two strange men, the Buick, and the driver in South Braintree Square not long before the shooting. He had spoken to the two men and thought he could identify any of them; he was not called at the trial. Donald Wight, a teller in the Braintree National Bank, gave a detailed description of two suspicious characters who had come into the bank at about 2:20; the description matched DeForrest's testimony very closely. He was never called.[53] Some of these witnesses were among those who came to Brockton to identify Sacco and Vanzetti after their arrest but failed to identify them.[54] Another witness, one Candido Di Bona, came forth with an affidavit on 8 August 1927, just before the execution. Employed by Slater and Morrill at the time of the crime, he claimed to have seen four men loitering on Pearl Street shortly before the crime and to have spoken to the two men loitering by the fence, the men who eventually attacked Parmenter and Berardelli. One of them had actually asked him when the payroll was coming. He had seen many pictures of Sacco and Vanzetti, and they did not resemble the men he had seen.[55]

Next come the eyewitnesses to the shooting itself, to whom we shall have occasion to return in another even more important connection. James McGlone, a teamster, saw the shooting from directly across the street. At the inquest he doubted he could identify either of the bandits, and he declined to identify either Sacco or Vanzetti at the trial. James Bostock, a Slater and Morrill repairman, saw most of the shooting from about sixty feet up Pearl Street, toward the crossing; to the Pinkertons he gave good descriptions of both bandits and picked a photo of Palmisano out of a group of pictures as "an excellent likeness" of one of the men. He did not identify either Sacco or Vanzetti at the trial. Lewis Wade, whom we have already discussed, saw the shooting from about sixty to one hundred feet in the other direction and, as we have seen, identified neither bandit. Annie Nichols, a rather strange witness, had testified at the inquest that she had seen most of the shooting and had seen a stocky bandit shoot Berardelli from her house two hundred feet back from the opposite side of the street. At the trial she backtracked, implying that she had seen much less, and said she could make no attempt to identify either man.[56]

Four witnesses saw the shooting from the Rice and Hutchins factory building directly opposite. Three of them—Sam Akeke and Patrick Walsh, who testified at the inquest, and Edgar Langlois, who testified at the inquest and the trial—said they could not identify either bandit.[57] A fourth, Barbara Liscomb, said she had seen one man very clearly and that he was neither of the defendants.[58] And three laborers who had been working on an excavation across the street—Pedro Iscorla, Henry

Cerro, and Sibriano Gudierres—testified that they had seen the shooting of Berardelli. Their accounts are frequently inconsistent with those of other witnesses, but all said that the bandit they saw was neither Sacco nor Vanzetti.[59] Eight witnesses to the shooting who had described the bandits could not identify Sacco and Vanzetti; only Pelser, who had never given any description until the trial, identified Sacco.

Last, twenty witnesses who saw the getaway car, all of whom had looked at the driver, the man leaning out with a revolver, or both, stated that they had seen neither Sacco nor Vanzetti in the car. They contrast with Splaine, Devlin, and Goodridge, who had identified Sacco in the car for the prosecution, and Levangie and Reed, who had placed Vanzetti either driving or in the front seat. Most of these witnesses saw the car around the South Braintree railroad crossing. They included Roy Gould, a salesman, who took a bullet through his overcoat from the man next to the driver and gave his story to the police but was never called. Later he swore an affidavit that the man who fired at him at a distance of ten feet was definitely not Sacco.[60] A glassblower, Frank Burke, testified that a bandit moved from the back seat to the front seat as the car approached the crossing, leaned out, pointed a revolver at Burke from a distance of a few feet, and yelled, "Get out of my way, you son of a B," in English. He also gave a good description of another bandit in the back of the car. He had seen Sacco, Vanzetti, and Orciani at Brockton, where he had once been associated with the police, immediately after their arrest. He said the defendants were not the men he had seen.[61] One of the defense witnesses, one Nicolo Gatti, had actually known Sacco in Milford some years before. He had not seen him in the car.[62]

Eyewitness testimony is notoriously fallible; physical and circumstantial evidence are far more important. Yet the testimony of the eyewitnesses to the crime remains significant. Over 75 percent of those having an opportunity to view the bandits before, during, or immediately after the crime denied having seen Sacco or Vanzetti. Of the eleven prosecution witnesses who did identify them, the testimony of eight of them—including *every single identifying witness to the crime or the escape*—was vitally impeached, either by their companions at the time of the shooting (Andrews, Pelser, and Goodridge); by their own statements on previous occasions (Andrews, Pelser, Splaine, and Devlin); by documentary evidence (Faulkner); by inherent impossibilities in their statements (Reed, who stated Vanzetti spoke clear and unmistakable English); or by the prosecution itself (Levangie, whose identification of Vanzetti as the driver was specifically disavowed by Katzmann). Only by dint of enormous effort did Katzmann, Williams, and Stewart manage to secure the eleven identifications they had. When individuals gave tentative identifications, they kept after them until they became more positive. When their stories included discrepancies, they smoothed them out.

The character of the prosecution's witnesses also raises questions. Was it merely a coincidence that the prosecution's most crucial witnesses included Andrews, a former prostitute; Goodridge, a habitual criminal who committed perjury when he gave his name; Pelser, whom the defense discovered a few years later in an alcoholic stupor in a run-down lodging house; Levangie, whose identification the Pinkertons had discounted at once, well before Vanzetti's arrest; and Splaine, whose boss described her as one of the most irresponsible people he had ever come in contact with? Is it not more likely that only witnesses such as these could be counted on to produce the testimony that would convict the two men? If eyewitness testimony has any meaning at all, one must conclude that the sum total of the eyewitness testimony in the case of Sacco and Vanzetti tends to exonerate the defendants. It also casts the gravest doubts upon the prosecution's construction of its case.

6 / The Defendants

The second type of evidence used to convict Sacco and Vanzetti was referred to by Judge Thayer as evidence of consciousness of guilt. It involved three major questions relating to their conduct during and after their arrest. First, the prosecution argued that the explanations they gave for their presence in West Bridgewater both on the night of their arrest and during their trial were false and thus at the very least tended to undermine their credibility. Second, the prosecution alleged that they had both attempted to draw their guns on the way to the police station when they were arrested on the night of 5 May. Last, the prosecution alleged that they had told many lies in their statements to Katzmann on 6 May, including some lies related to the South Braintree crime. Judge Thayer, both in his charge to the jury and in his subsequent denial of some defense motions for a new trial, laid great stress on the evidence of consciousness of guilt. From a legal standpoint, new evidence regarding the defendants' actions and statements at the time of their arrest tends deeply to undermine this part of the prosecution's case. From a historical standpoint, the whole issue of consciousness of guilt raises the question of the actual motives, activities, and character of the two defendants.

When Sacco and Vanzetti took the stand in their own defense, Katzmann devoted a large portion of his very lengthy cross-examination to various lies that he claimed they had told him during interrogations on 6 May, the day after their arrest. Legally, such lies had a dual significance: they tended to impeach the defendants' credibility as witnesses upon their own behalf, and if any of them related directly to the crime for which they were charged, they would constitute evidence of consciousness of guilt. Katzmann took particular care to establish that the defendants told lies relating to the South Braintree crime. In so doing, he read from purported transcripts of his May interrogations of the defendants—transcripts he declined to introduce in evidence. The state police files contain transcripts of Sacco and Vanzetti's answers to his questions, and the grand jury transcript also indicates some of what they actually said. These transcripts differ from the statements Katzmann read at the trial in several crucial respects.

Vanzetti, to begin with, had told Katzmann that he had bought his revolver in the North End of Boston several years previously for eighteen dollars. This was not true; he now said that he had bought it from a friend, Luigi Falzini, only a few months before. He had denied that he knew Boda or that he had seen a motorcycle on the night of 5 May or at Sacco's house, where Orciani had visited, on the previous day. He said that he had known Sacco for only a year and a half. On the stand he argued that he had been trying to shield his friends (Falzini, Boda, and Orciani) and to conceal his draft-evading excursion to Mexico with Sacco in 1917. He had also told Katzmann that he did not know what he had been doing on 15 April, while adding that he had been peddling fish on most days in April. This, too, was untrue, since he had gone to New York in the last week of April, but his concealment of his trip is consistent with his general attempt to hide his anarchist associations.[1]

Katzmann distorted Vanzetti's original responses twice during his cross-examination. Vanzetti had told him that on the previous Sunday, 2 May, he had slept in Boston. In the courtroom Katzmann quoted a transcript as follows: "Is that the only time while you lived in Plymouth that you ever slept in Boston? A. Yes, that is the only time I remember. I am not exactly sure." Vanzetti said that he did not remember that answer. He was right. In the original notes Vanzetti gives a completely different response: "I do not go to Boston very often. I don't think I slept in Boston last Sunday night. I have slept in Boston a few times since I have lived in Plymouth in the last six years." Katzmann continued that he had chided Vanzetti for his failure to remember where he had slept only four nights before and quoted Vanzetti as saying "I am ashamed. Q. What are you ashamed of? You have not been telling us the truth? A. Yes." In Dedham Katzmann continued:

> Q. Do you remember that? A. Well, I remember something like that.
> Q. There is one part of that, Mr. Vanzetti, you remember well, isn't there? A. Yes, sir. You want me to tell in this court now?
> Q. Don't you want me to ask you, sir? A. I don't say that. You can ask me very well. That depends on you.
> Q. Well, if you put it up to my generosity, Mr. Vanzetti, I won't ask you. A. Well—(rest of witness's reply unintelligible to stenographer).[2]

What Vanzetti actually said, his interrogation shows, is that he was ashamed because he had spent the night with a woman of easy virtue. Katzmann twisted this in court to imply that he told a lie.[3]

Sacco had also denied that he had been at the Johnson house or that he had ever been to Orciani's house or that he knew Boda—all lies that, like Vanzetti's, could be explained by his desire to shield his friends.[4] Sacco also admitted on cross-examination that he had lied on 6 May about where he had bought his revolver. This lie is more difficult to explain; his eventual story was that he bought it in a store in Milford. Most important, however, were Sacco's statements about his whereabouts on 15 April, since any lie about his whereabouts on the day of the crime could be used to indicate consciousness of guilt. During cross-examination Katzmann quoted Sacco as having said that he had read about the South Braintree robbery in the paper at work the next day. He continued to quote his interrogation of 6 May: Q. Were you working the day before you read it in the papers? A. I think I did. Q. Well, do you know? A. Sure." Again and again he stressed that answer, claiming it represented a lie as to Sacco's whereabouts on 15 April.[5] But the original transcript shows that Sacco discussed his whereabouts twice during the interrogation without giving such a specific denial. What he said is as follows.

> I don't remember when Patriot's Day was [Patriot's Day,
> 19 April, is a Massachusetts state holiday.] I loafed quite a few half
> days in April to get this passport. . . . about three weeks ago I began
> to inquire about the passport. . . . I took a whole day off in April to
> look for my passport; I think either Tuesday or Wednesday. I don't
> remember either the fifth or eighth of April or the tenth. In April
> I lost a day to fill out the income tax. There was only one single
> day that I lost the whole day's work to inform myself in regard to
> the passport. I think it was the beginning of the month of April,
> ever since I received a letter from home and then I started to in-
> vestigate about the passport. . . . I don't read English very good,
> but there was bandits in Braintree and I think it was at Rice &
> Hutchins. I read it the next day in the shop with some of the
> friends. I think I was working the day before I read it in the paper.
> I don't remember for sure if I stayed out half a day. I think I worked
> Thursday.[6]

The transcript of the grand jury hearing indicates that Sacco was far more specific even than this. After establishing with State Police Offi-cer Brouillard that Sacco and Vanzetti had been arrested on 5 May, Katz-mann continued:

Q. There was a conference at our office and the officers and the other one, a man named Occiani [*sic*], at the Police Station afterwards, was there? A. Yes, sir.

Q. They made a long statement which was taken down by a stenographer, did they? A. Yes.

Q. Did you hear them? A. Some of them, not all.

Q. At any time when in there did you hear Sacco say anything of where he was on the 15th of April? A. I did.

Q. What did he say? A. He said he was in Boston.

Q. Anything else? A. Making some arrangement about his passport.

Q. To go where? A. To go to Italy.[7]

If Brouillard's September 1920 statement is to be believed, Sacco told the same story on 6 May that he did at the trial.

Under the law only falsehoods bearing some relation to the crime committed could show consciousness of guilt. Yet this passage from the grand jury shows that Sacco simply did not make the most damaging statement attributed to him—namely, that he had been working on 15 April. The hypothesis that the two men were fearful of exposing themselves or their friends to prosecution or deportation as anarchists or bombers does explain almost all the lies they told. We shall shortly discuss their specific motives for concealment.

These lies in themselves might not have made much of an impression on the jury, but the police officers who arrested Sacco and Vanzetti added that their suspicious behavior was not confined to lying. Both of them, these officers testified, had attempted to draw their guns after being taken into custody. Many have argued that Sacco and Vanzetti's possession of weapons was in itself incriminating, even leaving aside the issue of their potential relationship to the South Braintree crime. But even Katzmann admitted that many Italians, anarchists or no, customarily carried weapons in that era.[8] Sacco had owned his automatic for years, and while his employer had cautioned him that he should get a permit for it, his possession of it did not in itself disturb him.[9] But had they attempted to draw their guns when arrested, this would indeed raise serious questions. And, despite their denials, even some sympathetic commentators on the case have seemed to assume that something like this did indeed take place. In fact, the whole story was a complete fabrication.

Like many other aspects of the prosecution's case, the contention that the two men had tried to draw their guns did not emerge until the trial. The police and prosecution staff, in giving reporters their firmly held opinion that they had found the South Braintree bandits in the days immediately following their arrest, never said anything to the press about any suspicious behavior at the time of their arrest. Nor did Brockton police officer Michael Connelly describe any suspicious movements when he described their arrest at Vanzetti's Plymouth trial. On 19 May 1921, however, Connelly gave Stewart a new statement. He explained that after receiving a call from police headquarters he had boarded the car coming from West Bridgewater. He had seen the two defendants seated in the last seat in the rear of the left-hand side of the car —on his right, that is—as he walked down the aisle. He continued:

> I asked where they came from; Vanzetti said "Bridgewater." Asked where he lived, he said "Plymouth." Asked Sacco and he said "Stoughton." Vanzetti dropped his hand down between himself and Sacco. At that point I took my revolver which I had in my hand, pointed it at them and told them they were under arrest. Officer Vaughn who came with me searched Vanzetti and found a 38 H & R revolver and five cartridges. This gun Vaughn handed to me.[10]

At the Dedham trial Connelly told an entirely different story.

> I went down through the car and when I got opposite to the seat I stopped and I asked them where they came from. They said "Bridgewater." I said, "What was you doing in Bridgewater?" They said, "We went down to see a friend of mine." I said, "Who is your friend?" He said, "A man by the—they call him 'Poppy.' " "Well," I said, "I want you, you are under arrest." Vanzetti was sitting on the inside of the seat.
> Q.[Williams] When you say "on the inside," you mean toward the aisle or toward the window? A. Toward the window. The inside of the car; and he went, put his hand in his hip pocket and I says, "Keep your hands out on your lap, or you will be sorry."
> THE DEFENDANT VANZETTI. You are a liar!
> THE WITNESS. . . . There was a revolver found on Vanzetti . . . [taken from his] left hip pocket, back pocket.[11]

Connelly's 19 May statement said nothing at all about any suspicious movements on Sacco's part. On the very same day, however, Stewart took a statement from another Brockton police officer, Merle Spear, who had driven Connelly, the defendants, and a third officer from the electric car to the Brockton police station. "I was considerably disturbed," he said, "by the way that Sacco kept moving his hands around on the way to the station and spoke two or three times to the officers, Shirley Snow and Mike Connelly, and asked them if they had cleaned him. They said that they had." Spear then said that Sacco's revolver had been discovered under his belt at the police station.[12]

At the trial Connelly expanded upon Spear's story. He now said that he had sat in the front seat facing the defendants and warned them that he would shoot if they made one false move. He then said that Sacco had reached under his overcoat twice and that he had warned him twice not to do so.[13] Spear completely changed his story so as to fit Connelly's. He denied having seen the defendants during the ride himself at all but confirmed that Connelly had told Sacco to keep his hands where he could see them.[14] Officer Snow was not called.

What actually happened had been described by Connelly before the grand jury nine months earlier, on 10 September 1920. He began by describing how he had boarded the streetcar.

Q. [Katzmann] As a result of what you had been told, what did you do? A. I placed two men,—two Italians, Vanzetti and Sacco, under arrest.

Q. Did you search them? A. I did.

Q. What did you find? A. *Further up the line another officer got on the car to help me, and we found two guns* [emphasis added]. [Description of guns follows.]

Q. Did you ask them where they had been? A. I asked them where they had come from.

Q. What did they say? A. From Bridgewater. I said, "Well, you are under arrest as suspicious persons, and we are going to hold you for the Bridgewater police."

Q. Did you have any talk with them? A. *No, I did not have any talk with them until we got up to the central station* [emphasis added].

Q. Did you then? A. Yes.

Q. What was it? A. I asked where they lived, and Sacco said he lived in Stoughton and Vanzetti said he lived in Plymouth.

Q. Go on. A. *That is all I had to do with it* [emphasis added].[15]

After the trial, a Brockton police officer named Curran told a defense investigator that several of his fellow officers were no longer speaking to Connelly because of his testimony. The original source for this information was Shirley Snow, the officer who had been with Connelly on the streetcar but evidently declined to testify.[16] The statements of Connelly and Spear, like the testimony of identification witnesses like Pelser, Andrews, and Dolbeare, represented a desperate last-minute attempt by the prosecution to beef up its case. Their effect upon the jury is unknown, but Judge Thayer, in his charge, made an obvious attempt to impress the jury with the significance of the offier's testimony.

> The defendants have testified that nothing of that kind happened. Again, what is the truth? . . . if you find Vanzetti did so intend to use his revolver, that is evidence tending to prove self-consciousness of guilt of some crime committed by him. If it proves such self-consciousness, then you will naturally ascertain the nature, character and gravity of the crime committed. If a person is willing to use a deadly weapon such as a revolver upon an arresting officer in order to gain his liberty, you have a right to ask what would naturally be the nature, character and gravity of the crime committed.[17]

The prosecution's attempt to use Sacco and Vanzetti's statements against them, then, rested largely upon falsification of their statements, while the accusation that they had tried to use their weapons rested upon thin air. Yet the fact remains that the two men *did* lie about the reasons for their presence in Bridgewater on the night of their arrest on 5 and 6 May and that they did not tell the whole truth even at the trial. Their motives relate to the anarchist background to the case, which we have already discussed in connection with their arrest and which will also serve to introduce some discussion of the two men's character.

After their arrest Sacco and Vanzetti told Stewart and Katzmann that they had been in West Bridgewater to visit a friend of Vanzetti's named Pappi. They denied that they had been at the Johnson house or even that they knew Boda or Orciani. At the Dedham trial they admitted that this was false and claimed that they had gone to the Johnson garage with Boda and Orciani because they wanted Boda's car to collect anarchist literature and hide it in a safe place. Vanzetti said that a group of anarchists had met on Sunday 24 April, in East Boston and decided that he should go to New York to investigate the fate of two friends, Roberto Elia and Andrea Salsedo, who had been arrested there. He left that night and returned on Thursday, 29 April, when he took a boat from New York, alighted at Providence, Rhode Island, and took a train home. On the evening of Sunday, 2 May, he had met his friends in Boston again. Sacco said that Vanzetti had told the meeting that no one in New York knew why Salsedo and Elia had been arrested but that they feared the presence of a spy within their group who would betray everyone who had contributed money for Salsedo and Elia's defense.[18] On 5 May they had gone out to find the literature and look for a place to hide it.

Interviewed in Italy in 1928, Mike Boda, whose real name was Mario Buda, confirmed that they had planned to collect literature and added that they would have taken it to Providence. Providence *was* a center of Galleanisti activity—according to some police reports, the presses of the *Cronaca Sovversiva* had been taken there after Galleani's arrest—and the literature would presumably have been given to friends whom Vanzetti had seen on his way back from New York. Boda also confirmed that they had feared the presence of a police spy within their group.[19] A letter written by Vanzetti to Aldino Felicani shortly before his arrest confirms, in rather cryptic terms, that he, too, had felt such fears about an unnamed comrade.[20] But in other ways this story has never been fully convincing. In particular, if in fact the anarchists were acting on instructions received by Vanzetti in New York, why did they wait three or four days? Vanzetti further muddied the waters by saying that they feared further large-scale police raids upon anarchists on 1 May—but, according to him, the decision to collect literature had not been taken until 2 May.

As a matter of fact, the defendants did not tell the whole truth. As we have seen, the event that led to their outing on the night of 5 May was almost certainly *not* Vanzetti's trip to New York but rather the news of Salsedo's suicide and the government's announcement—published in Boston newspapers—that the Galleanisti bore the responsibility for the 1919 bombings. As it was, Vanzetti mentioned the suicide only briefly on *redirect* examination, and Sacco did not mention it at all. The defendants decided—possibly in consultation with their attorneys but probably on their own—partially to conceal their real motives. The reason seems simple enough. To have admitted that the press reports of 4 May had galvanized them into action would implicitly have admitted that the government's accusation was true. Galleanisti from the Boston area probably *had* helped carry out the June 1919 bombings, including Carlo Valdinocci, whom both men knew well.[21]

On the night of 5 May, Sacco, Vanzetti, Orciani, and Boda evidently feared an imminent federal descent upon all Galleanisti remaining at large. Their arrest may easily have convinced Sacco and Vanzetti that such a roundup was indeed taking place. Chief Stewart's initial interrogation of the two men on the night of 5 May must have tended to confirm these suspicions. Stewart asked the two men what they had been doing in Bridgewater, whether they knew Boda, Coacci, or another man he called Erico Parkoi, and whether they were anarchists, Communists, or belonged to any "clubs or societies." Both men made up a story about visiting a friend of Vanzetti's, denied knowing any of their friends, and confessed only to some vague, limited sympathy for anarchism.[22] Stewart on the night of 5 May did not ask either man any questions related to the South Braintree crime. The next day Katzmann did not ask about the defendants' whereabouts on 15 April until well into his interrogation of the two men.

For all that, Sacco and Vanzetti's behavior and anarchist associations raise important questions. What exactly does this evidence, combined with what we know from other sources, tell us about the two men? No clear answer is possible; too many authors on both sides of the case have fallen into the trap of attempting to exonerate or to convict them on the basis of spotty character evidence. Yet, while the character of Sacco and Vanzetti cannot be the determining factor in an analysis of their guilt or innocence, it is too important an issue to be ignored.

It is also an interesting issue because both men present remarkable contradictions. On the one hand, as Nunzio Pernicone has pointed out, they were clearly dedicated revolutionaries.[23] Both had been active in strikes—Sacco in Milford, Vanzetti in Plymouth in the strike at the great cordage plant in 1916. Their leader Galleani was a fervent adherent of political violence who for years circulated a manual on making bombs. In 1917 they had followed Galleani's advice and fled to Mexico rather than register for the draft. They too *could* have been involved in the 1919 bombings, although no direct evidence suggests that they were. Other bombings took place after Sacco and Vanzetti's arrest, including the bombing of a juror's home in 1927 and the bombing of Judge Thayer's home in 1932. Sacco and Vanzetti, in short, belonged to a group that believed in violent action to achieve political change. They may have been involved in such violence themselves, and on the night of 5 May they may have been trying to hide evidence of bombings. On the other hand, Pernicone has pointed out that there is virtually no evidence of any *banditry* having been committed by Italian-American anarchists.

It is not possible to make any definitive judgment of Sacco and Vanzetti's guilt or innocence based on our scattered bits of knowledge of their earlier lives, their political associations, and their behavior after their arrest, but it is safe to say that each of them, in his own way, makes a rather unlikely bandit. Vanzetti has particularly appealed to most students of the case, as well as to many of those who were involved in it. Clearly a man of great warmth and intelligence, he seems before his arrest to have had many friends and few enemies. Even a Plymouth policeman was willing to testify for him at his Dedham trial. In prison he became remarkably eloquent, and he unceasingly proclaimed his innocence of any crime up until the moment of his electrocution. Thus, even Francis Russell, who has asserted—wrongly, as we shall see—that Vanzetti's revolver had probably been taken from Berardelli, maintains that Sacco had shot Berardelli, and even believes that Boda was involved in the Bridgewater and South Braintree crimes, still concludes on largely intuitive grounds that Vanzetti was completely innocent.

Sacco's personality has never exerted the same hold on intellectuals. Less articulate than Vanzetti, he abandoned hope in his cause early and refused to sign many motions or appeals for clemency on the grounds that capitalist courts would never give him justice. He resented many of his upper-class defenders and fired Moore in 1924, complaining about the activities of "all your philanthropist friends." Increasingly committed to anarchy during his years in prison, he could not understand those who saw his case in terms of abstract justice. Yet, to judge from his life before his arrest, Sacco seems in many ways a far less likely criminal than Vanzetti. Vanzetti was a dreamer and something of a drifter. Though as a fish peddler he was a fairly successful small businessman, he had the kind of philosophical but passionate nature that historically has often proved capable of political crimes.

Sacco, on the other hand, was in many ways a model of respectability. A highly skilled worker, he earned as much as eighty dollars a week as an edge trimmer at the 3-K shoe factory in Stoughton. His private passions were his wife, his son (a daughter was born after his arrest), and his vegetable garden. With his wife he participated in amateur dramatic

9. Bartolomeo Vanzetti and Nicola Sacco, *center*, apparently taken
during their trial in Dedham. (Courtesy Boston Public Library)

productions. Through work he had accumulated the extraordinary sum
of fifteen hundred dollars in a savings account—equivalent to about ten
thousand dollars today. His employers' respect and affection for him are
obvious from their testimony. Among his other duties, Sacco had sometimes entered the factory alone at night to check the fires. A January
1921 report by State Police Officer John Scott gives an interesting picture of the prospective defendant.

> Sacco has always had Socialistic Tendencies, and would argue
> Socialism to his friends and companions, but said he could not
> kill, the sight of blood made him sick, yet he had a loaded revolver
> and extra ammunition in his possession when arrested, and also
> a rifle in his house at the same time.
>
> Joseph Macone, Italian banker of Milford has known Sacco sev-
> eral years, says his reputation is good. Had Socialistic ideas but
> was never known to do any harm. Do not think he would have had
> the courage to commit such an act as the Braintree murder. Sacco
> has frequently sent money to his parents in Italy through
> Macones Bank. Very little can be learned against Sacco in Milford,
> all his friends are contributing to this defense fund.[24]

10. William G. Thompson, Herbert B. Ehrmann, and Thomas O'Connor leaving the statehouse in Boston, 1927.
(Courtesy Harvard Law School Library)

When Fred Moore left the defense in 1924 the Sacco-Vanzetti Defense Committee approached a conservative Boston trial lawyer, William G. Thompson, who had already helped argue some of the posttrial appeals. Evidently Thompson had not particularly enjoyed his associations with Moore and the defense committee, and when the latter came to ask him to take the case he asked for twenty-five thousand dollars in advance. He was not happy when they raised the money, but after talking with Vanzetti he became completely committed to his clients' cause. Certain that the two men were innocent, he sought to vindicate Massachusetts justice by winning them a new trial and an acquittal. He grew close to Vanzetti, who came to understand Thompson's legalistic approach and once said that had he had Thompson for a lawyer from the start he would never have been a convict. Thompson's relationship with Sacco was more difficult because Sacco regarded Thompson's attempts to save him from capitalist justice as doomed; Thompson in turn was roused to fury by Sacco's refusal even to observe formalities necessary for his defense. In an extraordinary and previously unpublished letter, Thompson explained his view of his clients and of the case to an old friend in November 1926.

These men were tried at a time when Mitchell Palmer had stirred up the whole country with fear and hatred of the so-called "Reds." . . . Both these men were half educated dreamers and fanatics, and believers in what they call Libertarianism, which is another name for anarchy. Vanzetti is the more intelligent of the two. They are great readers, and having no background of general education are easily swept off their feet by the eloquence or persuasiveness of such writers as Tolstoi, Prince Krapotkin [sic], Bakunin, Proudhon, and others. They do not seem to have felt the influence of American ideas in the slightest degree. They are thoroughly foreign, with the point of view of the European radical proletariat. It is my belief, based upon a long study of the case, that they had nothing whatever to do with the crime with which they are charged; but that they are the victims of the agitation engineered by Mitchell Palmer. Three or four of the affidavits filed in support of the last motion clearly show the activity of the Federal Department of Justice in the prosecution of these two men. Both of them want to be martyrs, and Sacco for two years has been especially desirous of having all defense dropped so that he may go to the electric chair as a martyr to what he calls "the Cause." I think it would be perfectly easy for me to get both of these men to write me a letter saying that they did not desire any further services from me or from any other lawyer.

But to my mind the execution of these men under the circumstances would be little short of a disaster. To myself, at least, I appear to be supporting the conservative interest in this case. Millions of people in this country and all over the world have come to believe that these men are the victims of capitalistic persecution. There is just enough truth in the charge to make it dangerous. Their adherents can never be convinced that it is not true, and if the men are executed, violent and permanent antagonisms will be created which will certainly not be conducive to social peace and good order, and may lead to serious consequences.

For these reasons I intend, despite misrepresentations of motives and personal abuse of all kinds, to stay in the case.[25]

All Thompson's efforts proved in vain, and when in August 1927 Governor Fuller and the Lowell Committee ruled that the two men were guilty he pulled out of the case, leaving others to argue the last-minute appeals. In the waning hours of the defendants' lives Felix

Frankfurter arranged for Vanzetti to send for Thompson, now resting in New Hampshire, in the hope that a further appeal from Thompson might sway the governor. These hopes were disappointed, but Thompson reappeared on death row only hours before the execution for one last talk with his clients. His conversation with Vanzetti began with some words about Vahey and Graham, the lawyers who had defended him in Plymouth and whom Vanzetti now bitterly reproached for poor advice and an inadequate defense.

> I then said to Mr. Vanzetti that although my belief in his inno-
> cence had all the time been strengthened, both by my study of the
> evidence, and by my increasing knowledge of his personality, yet
> there was a chance, however remote, that I might be mistaken,
> and that I thought he ought for my sake, in this closing hour of his
> life, when nothing could save him, to give me his most solemn re-
> assurance, both with respect to himself and to Sacco. Mr. Vanzetti
> then said to me quietly and calmly, and with a sincerity which I
> could not doubt, that I need have no worry about this matter; that
> both he and Sacco were absolutely innocent of the South Brain-
> tree crime; and that he (Vanzetti) was equally innocent of the
> Bridgewater crime; that while looking back he now realized more
> clearly than he ever had the grounds of the suspicion against him
> and Sacco, he felt that no allowance had been made for his igno-
> rance of American points of view and habits of thought, or for his
> fear as a Radical and almost as an outlaw; and that in reality he
> was convicted on evidence that would not have convicted him
> had he not been an anarchist; so that he was in a very real sense
> dying for his Cause.

Continuing, Thompson asked Vanzetti if he might make a public statement asking his friends not to retaliate against the execution by "violence and reprisal." When Vanzetti protested the injustices against him and declined to do so, Thompson asked whether "he did not prefer the prevalence of his opinions to the infliction of punishment upon persons, however richly he might think they deserved it. This led to a pause in the conversation."

Vanzetti added that all great altruistic movements became perverted by misunderstanding and self-interest, just as they met a violent response from established institutions. Even Christianity had begun "in simplicity and sincerity, which were met with persecution and tyranny; but . . . it later passed quietly into ecclesiasticism and tyranny." Denying this, Thompson referred to "the supreme confidence shown by Jesus in the truth of His own views by forgiving, even when on the cross, his enemies and persecutors." He urged Vanzetti to emulate this example, and Vanzetti, after a heated discussion, agreed to think about what Thompson had said. In the event, Vanzetti said, as he was strapped into the electric chair, that he wanted "to forgive some people for what they are doing to me." Thompson's account concludes:

> I then had a brief interview with Mr. Sacco, who lay upon a cot bed in the adjoining cell, and could easily have heard and undoubtedly did hear all of my conversation with Mr. Vanzetti. This conversation was very brief. Mr. Sacco arose from his cot; referred feelingly to some points of disagreement between us in the past; said he hoped that our differences of opinion had not affected our personal relations; thanked me for what I had done for him; showed no sign of fear; shook hands with me firmly, and bade me goodbye. His manner also was one of absolute sincerity. It was magnanimous in him not to refer in detail to our previous differences of opinion because at the root of it all lay his conviction, often expressed to me, that all efforts on his behalf, either in court or with public authorities, would be useless because no capitalistic society could afford to accord him justice. I had taken the contrary view; but at this last interview he did not suggest that the result justified his view and not mine.[26]

7 / *The Alibis*

oth Sacco and Vanzetti presented substantial alibis for 15 April when the defense put on its case. Alibi evidence is of course extremely difficult to evaluate. If a defendant has a documented alibi, like Orciani's work records at the foundry he worked in, he will not be charged with the crime in question. Otherwise his alibi is bound to depend on his own and others' recollections, and the other witnesses are likely to be friends and acquaintances whose testimony the prosecution can easily impugn. Sacco and Vanzetti's alibis were about as strong as they could possibly be, given the circumstances of their lives, although a notable proportion of Sacco's alibi witnesses were fellow anarchists whose motives are inevitably suspect.[1]

At the trial Vanzetti stuck by his statement to Katzmann on 5 May that he had been peddling fish on 15 April. He added that he had met one Joseph Rosen, a salesman who had offered him a piece of cloth, at about 11:30; that he had brought the cloth over to the home of Alfonsina Brini, with whom he had formerly boarded, to ask her opinion of it; that he later sold fish to a factory worker, Angel Guidobone; and that he spent over an hour between 2:00 and 3:30 talking to a fisherman, Melvin Corl, and that they spoke to a boatbuilder, Frank Jesse, during that time as well. All these witnesses corroborated what Vanzetti had said. As Katzmann naturally stressed, the issue of whether these incidents had actually taken place on 15 April was cloudier. The witnesses fixed the date in various ways. The most effective was Rosen, who testified that he had gone to Whitman, near South Braintree, late that afternoon and rented a room at a rooming house there for the night. A rooming house clerk confirmed that she had rented a room for that night.[2] Most of Vanzetti's alibi witnesses, then, were neither anarchists nor Italians.

Sacco's alibi was much more detailed. Having told Katzmann on 6 May that he might have been in Boston to check on his passport on 15 April, he confirmed this at the trial. Nine defense witnesses corroborated his account of his movements on that day. Dominic Ricci, a carpenter, saw Sacco at the railroad station in Stoughton and testified that Sacco said he was going to Boston. A contractor, Angelo Monello, testified to meeting Sacco at 11:00 A.M. on Hanover Street in the North End of Boston. Albert Bosco, editor of the Italian daily *La Notizia*, recalled meeting Sacco at dinner (lunch in modern parlance) at Boni's restaurant between 11:30 and 1:00. An Italian journalist, Felice Guadenagi, who worked for the *Gazetta del Massachusetts*, and an advertising broker, John D. Williams, who sold ads to foreign newspapers, both said they had joined Bosco and Sacco in the restaurant. Sacco said he reached the Italian consulate on Berkeley Street around 2:00 and presented a photograph of his family to get a passport to return to Italy but was refused because the photograph was too large. On 11 May 1921 Giuseppe Andrower, who had been an officer of the Italian consulate in Boston in April 1920, deposed that Sacco had indeed come in that day with an overlarge photograph.[3] Another Italian official, Rafaele Murdulo, told a defense investigator in April 1921 that he remembered Sacco's overlarge photograph; it is not clear why he was not called.[4]

Returning to the North End to spend the afternoon, Sacco met Guadenagi again in a coffeehouse. Antonio Dentamore, who was both the foreign exchange manager of the Haymarket National Bank and an ordained Catholic priest, testified to meeting Sacco there as well. An Italian grocer, Carlos Affe, confirmed that between 3:00 and 4:00 Sacco had visited him and paid him fifteen dollars for groceries he had bought in March.[5] Then, Sacco said, he walked to South Station and took his train home.

As in Vanzetti's case, two key questions arise with respect to Sacco's alibi: the character of the alibi witnesses and their ability to fix the date of their meetings with him. Of Sacco's alibi witnesses, one, Guadenagi, was a member of the Sacco-Vanzetti Defense Committee, a fact that clearly cuts both ways, since his sympathy for the defendant would have been entirely natural had he known him from his own experience to be innocent. *La Notizia* and the *Gazetta del Massachusetts*, which employed Bosco and Guadenagi, were not anarchist papers; both were extremely conservative. But the carpenter Ricci and the grocer Affe were both subscribers to the *Cronaca Sovversiva* and therefore presumably anarchists. Ricci had lived in Somerville, Massachusetts, at the same address as Carlo Vandinocci, thought by some to have blown himself up in the 2 June 1919 bombing of A. Mitchell Palmer's house.[6] Authorities also identified John Williams as a "prominent I.W.W. and socialist speaker."[7] It is natural for people of like belief to associate with one another, and a Republican's alibi witnesses are likely to be mostly Republicans. At the same time it is easy to see why Fred Moore reportedly was skeptical about some of Sacco's alibi witnesses.[8] Herbert Ehrmann also betrayed some skepticism about Ricci's testimony.[9] Ricci had aroused Moore's suspicions when he first told him his story before the trial. Sacco said from the beginning that he had taken a train shortly before 9:00, but Ricci told Moore that he had seen him at 7:00 A.M.[10]

The issue of whether the witnesses might have seen Sacco on a different day is considerably easier in his case than Vanzetti's. While the occurrences Vanzetti described could have taken place on virtually any day in early April 1920, there were very few days on which Sacco's witnesses could have seen him in Boston. By his own account he went to Boston on three separate occasions to look into his passport—in mid or late March, not long after hearing that his mother had died; on 15 April, when he found the picture was too large; and on 4 May, when he brought a new photograph and received a "Foglio di Via," a simpler form of passport.[11]

There seems to be no question that Sacco *did* at one point present an oversize photograph at the consulate. A photographer, Edward Maertens, had records to show that he had taken a seven-by-nine picture of the Sacco family on Sunday, 21 March. This picture had been delivered to Sacco on 3 April. Maertens had taken another passport-size photo of the family sometime during April but could not fix the date.[12] These dates are consistent with Sacco's having initially inquired about the passport in late March and having brought the large picture in on 15 April. But since Sacco's employer thought he might have been out a day or part of a day in the week before (his memory was unsure on this point), it is possible that Sacco had taken the oversize photograph to the consulate before 15 April.[13] The critical issue, indeed, is that of the other day that Sacco took off. Perhaps it was in late March, and on that day he went to the consulate and learned that he must bring in a photograph. Or, it may have been in early April, in which case it might have been on *that* occasion that Sacco found that his photograph was too large, leaving his whereabouts on 15 April unaccounted for. Although both Andrower and Murdulo claimed to remember that Sacco had brought his photograph in on 15 April, their memories cannot be trusted entirely on this point.

Sacco himself was rather vague on this point when interrogated by Katzmann on 6 May, the day after his arrest. The transcript of his statements reads as follows.

... I loafed quite a few half days in April to get this passport. I begin to think of going back to the old country a month ago, when I received a letter from there, about three weeks ago I began to inquire about the passport. . . . I took a whole day off in April to look for my passport; I think either Tuesday or Wednesday. I don't remember either the fifth or eighth of April or the tenth. In April I lost a day to fill out the income tax. There was only one single day that I lost the whole day's work to inform myself in regard to the passport. I think it was the beginning of the month of April, ever since I received a letter from home and then I started to investigate about the passport. . . . I read in the Boston Post there was bandit—robbing money over near Rice & Hutchins. . . . I read it the next day in the shop with some of the friends. I think I was working the day before I read it in the paper. I don't remember for sure if I stayed out half a day. I think I worked Thursday.[14]

One of the most frustrating features of the case is the apparent failure either of the defense or of the prosecution to attempt to verify Sacco's alibi in the immediate aftermath of his arrest. The testimony of the Italian consular officials would have been worth a great deal more in the immediate aftermath of the crime, and the issue of Sacco's other day off might easily have been cleared up. We have no evidence, however, of either prosecution or defense contacts with the consulate or with Sacco's employers for many months. Sacco's story, then, is plausible but not definitely proven.

In fixing the date of their meetings with Sacco, Bosco, Guadenagi, and Dentamore recalled that at that time they had all discussed a banquet being given for James T. Williams, Jr., editor of the ultraconservative *Boston Evening Transcript*, by Italian Franciscans in the North End. Only Dentamore attended the banquet, which the defense proved years later had actually taken place by producing a description of it in *La Notizia* for 16 April.[15] Guadenagi and Bosco, who had not attended it, wrongly remembered that it had been scheduled for that evening: Dentamore testified correctly that he had attended it at noontime. Williams, the advertising broker, stated emphatically that he always went to pick up ads in the North End on Thursdays and that he recalled seeing his doctor the same day. His doctor's records showed that he had treated Williams on 15 April. He had not seen him on any other day during April or on any of the other days that Sacco had been in Boston.[16] The grocer, Affe, produced a record showing that Sacco had bought fifteen dollars worth of groceries on credit on 20 March (a Saturday) and paid for them in cash on 15 April; Katzmann subsequently suggested to the jury that this entry in the book was not in Affe's handwriting.[17] Either these witnesses were telling the truth, or they all collaborated in a complicated fabrication.

Sacco's last alibi witness ranks with John W. Faulkner, who claimed to have seen Vanzetti get off his train in East Braintree, as one of the two most extraordinary witnesses of the entire trial. James M. Hayes was a mason and a contractor and a former highway surveyor of the town of Stoughton, where Sacco lived. A defense investigator had apparently consulted him on another matter in early 1921, and he had helped the investigator find a Stoughton laborer, Wilson Dorr, who testified to having seen the murder car for the defense.[18] The defense also consulted him for some unspecified purpose during the first few days of the trial, and he attended the trial once or twice with his wife. Sacco claimed in subsequent testimony that he recognized Hayes as having been on the train with him returning to Stoughton on 15 April.

Hayes now explained that with the help of a time book with which he kept track of his work he had determined that he had indeed taken the train to and from Boston on 15 April 1920. Among other things, he recalled injuring himself early that week, he remembered working on his car, and he remembered that on the morning of 15 April his brother gave him fifty dollars, part of which he used to buy parts in Boston. Sacco, recalled to the stand, explained how he had recognized Hayes. Katzmann, cross-examining Sacco out of Hayes's presence, asked him various questions about the trip; Sacco could not answer several of them but said that he had sat on the right-hand side of the car and had seen Hayes across the aisle. Hayes was recalled and told Katzmann that he had sat on the left-hand side of the car.[19] The story seems too good to be true, and apparently it was. According to Upton Sinclair, Moore subsequently told him that Hayes's story was a fabrication.[20] An undated note in Moore's pretrial papers refers to Hayes as "a Communist who doesn't believe Sacco is guilty," and a desperate Fred Moore apparently yielded to temptation in an effort to strengthen his case.[21]

That Moore and the defense committee felt it necessary to bolster Sacco's alibi with Hayes, and conceivably with other perjured witnesses as well, does not mean that the essence of his story was not true. Just as the prosecution might not quibble over the quality of evidence used to convict two men they believed to be guilty, the defense may have taken liberties to exonerate two men they believed to be innocent. The evidence with respect to Sacco's alibi is tantalizing, suggesting that he was at the consulate on 15 April while leaving open a loophole broad enough to create the possibility that he was lying. *If* he was lying, however, one must conclude that several of his alibi witnesses knowingly collaborated in a complete fabrication. The two men's alibis for 15 April do not settle anything; neither, certainly, is as strong as Vanzetti's alibi for 24 December. The truth must be sought elsewhere.

8 / *Vanzetti's Gun*

The most serious evidence and the only physical evidence produced by the prosecution to connect Vanzetti to the South Braintree crime was the .38 caliber Harrington and Richardson revolver found upon him at the time of his arrest.[1] Harold Williams did not attempt to tie this gun to the crime in his opening statement, but during the trial the prosecution elaborated a claim that this revolver had formerly belonged to the slain guard Alessandro Berardelli and that it had been taken from him in the course of the robbery. In support of this claim they produced evidence showing that Berardelli had owned and habitually carried a Harrington and Richardson revolver, that it had recently been repaired, and that Vanzetti's gun showed evidence of one of the repairs that had been made upon it. In response the defense called Luigi Falzini, who claimed to have bought the revolver from Ricardo Orciani in October 1919 and sold it to Vanzetti in January or February 1920; Rexford Slater, who testified that he had received the gun from his mother-in-law roughly in 1918, when she came to Massachusetts from Maine, and sold it to Orciani, with whom he had worked, in the fall of 1919; and Eldridge Atwater, Slater's brother-in-law, who testified that the gun had belonged to his father-in-law and that his mother-in-law had taken it to Massachusetts some years earlier.[2] Falzini, Slater, and Atwater all identified the gun, and Slater and Atwater also identified the case that went with it. The defense did not call Orciani. Despite some holes and contradictions in the prosecution's argument, the juryman John Dever was persuaded that Vanzetti's gun had been taken from Berardelli,[3] which suggests that the rest of the jury was similarly convinced. But documents newly released from the state police files show that Vanzetti's revolver was very definitely *not* Berardelli's. What is equally significant is that they show that the prosecution sent Vanzetti to the electric chair on evidence they knew to be false.

The prosecution's argument that Vanzetti's gun had been taken from Berardelli during the shooting was always shaky because no eyewitness saw anything like that take place. Lewis Wade thought he saw Berardelli *reaching* for his revolver but did not claim to see the gun itself. Witnesses described the bandits shooting and picking up the payroll boxes but not taking anything from either of the bodies.[4]

Indeed, the prosecution could not definitely show that Berardelli had been armed at the time of the robbery at all. At the inquest the Slater and Morrill superintendent Thomas Fraher stated that while he "could not say positively" that Berardelli was armed, "I have seen him in the factory day after day with a revolver and he always carried it to my knowledge," and added that Parmenter always carried a revolver as well.[5] James Bostock, a machinist and eyewitness to the shooting, testified on direct examination in Dedham that he knew Berardelli carried a revolver and thought he had seen it on the Saturday night before the shooting, but on cross-examination he said he had only seen the gun once, in the morning, sometime before.[6] The claim that Berardelli was armed may have originated because Slater and Morrill had a pecuniary interest in showing that at least one of the guards had carried a weapon. Their payroll insurance policy specified that the payroll should be carried by two guards in an automobile.[7] On his deathbed Parmenter told a doctor that on 15 April he had asked Mr. Slater for his car but that Slater had replied, "Go ahead, never mind the car."[8] Although the insurance company's files relating to the claim have been destroyed, it was customary, in cases where the insured party had not fully carried out the terms of the policy, to pay a percentage of the loss. The percentage would reflect the ratio of the premium actually paid *to the premium that would had to have been paid to secure a policy that would have covered the conditions under which the loss took place.* In fact, during the preparation for the trial a defense investigator learned that the company had imposed a penalty of three thousand dollars in settling the claim.

Not until January 1921, when a trial date had finally been set, did Chief Stewart begin looking into the history of Berardelli's gun. Three Slater and Morrill employees confirmed that Berardelli carried a revolver, and Superintendent Fraher said that it was a "cylinder pistol" of, he thought, .32 caliber. On 31 January Stewart interviewed Berardelli's widow, Sarah. She said that her husband had received a gun from Parmenter when he began carrying the payroll. From her statements to Stewart and to Katzmann the following month it is clear that he had initially come to Slater and Morrill about a year before the shooting as an employee of a detective agency, to investigate internal theft. He had been hired by Slater and Morrill as a permanent employee about six months before his death. Sarah Berardelli definitely stated that he had not had the gun when he first began working there but that Parmenter had given it to him later when he began guarding the payroll. She told both Stewart and Katzmann that she had helped take in the gun for repairs about a month before the shooting. Berardelli had given Parmenter the claim check, and she did not know if he had ever gotten the gun back. She did not recognize a gun shown her as her husband's and said that she could not even remember its color; she had refused to let him bring it into their house, perhaps because of their two small children.[9]

A few days later Stewart went with Mrs. Berardelli to Boston, where she identified the Iver Johnson Company as the shop to which she and her husband had taken the revolver. At the Iver Johnson Company a Mr. Jones found a record showing that Berardelli had indeed brought a gun in on the twentieth of March. The downstairs records listed it as a .38 caliber Harrington and Richardson revolver like Vanzetti's; the repair records upstairs stated that it had received a new hammer and listed it as a .32 caliber revolver. There was no record of its being delivered, but Mr. Jones stated it had probably been picked up. Stewart returned to Iver Johnson with Vanzetti's revolver a few days later and asked Mr. Jones whether its hammer was new. Mr. Jones said, "after looking it over carefully, that he thought it was but that he was not so sure of it that he cared to testify in court." According to Stewart's memorandum, Jones said that the downstairs record was more likely to be accurate as to the caliber, "for the reason that the receiving clerk copies from the gun itself the make, calibre, etc. and that the repairman upstairs on that particular gun would have no occasion to do so as a 32 calibre is built on the same size frame as a 38 and takes the same kind and size of hammer." Such speculation left open the possibility that Vanzetti's gun was the gun in question, but it is not very convincing. The main difference between a .32 and a .38 is that the former holds six bullets and the latter five; a repairman would presumably be as likely to notice the difference as a clerk.[10]

Stewart brought in the gun and met George Fitzmeyer, the repairman who had worked on Berardelli's gun. Stewart's 18 February memorandum describes what followed:

> He [Fitzmeyer] was shown the gun and asked to take it apart.
> I then asked him if that was a new spring, pointing to the spring of
> the gun and he said "No that is not a new spring." I said "What
> about the hammer?" looked at the hammer and he said "It is
> a new hammer." Asked him how he knew and he said that the
> notch on the back of the hammer which might be called the spring
> notch shows no sign of wear and the general appearance of the

hammer itself would indicate that it was a new hammer. He further stated that the case hardening or finish on the hammer which is done with bone dust has only been used by the Harrington and Richardson Firearms Company for two or three years at the outside and that the gun itself cylinder and barrel, showed that it was a much older gun than that.

In answer to the question "Then in your opinion there is no question but what this is a new hammer?" said "There is no question at all about it."[11]

Taking the revolver apart under these uncontrolled conditions constituted illegal tampering with evidence, which today would be powerful grounds for a mistrial. More significant with respect to the guilt or innocence of Vanzetti are Fitzmeyer's conclusions. His identification of the hammer as new was based largely on the use of a new finish upon it, one that had been in use for two or three years. All this meant was that the hammer was new in the sense of not being the gun's original hammer; it did not mean that it had been put on in March 1920. What Fitzmeyer did not and could not say was that he had installed the hammer in 1920. Since he himself had listed Berardelli's revolver as a .32 in his records it would have been impossible for him to say so.

Fitzmeyer's testimony underwent changes in Dedham. Williams asked him a more leading question: "Q. Now, will you tell us if, in your opinion, any repairs have been made to that revolver recently? A. Well, a new hammer, I should call it, a new hammer. Q. And how can you tell that a new hammer has been put in there? A. Well, the firing pin does not show of ever being struck. There isn't any burnt mark or powder mark or anything on it." The difference in his explanation is striking and raises the possibility that the firing pin might simply have been cleaned. The defense missed a great opportunity by refusing to have Fitzmeyer's records introduced in evidence; as a result, he did not even have to account for his notation of the revolver he repaired as a .32 caliber. The prosecution also called Lincoln Wadsworth, who had made the downstairs notation of the gun as a .38. Six years later Wadsworth told the Lowell Committee that there were "thousands of times more chances" that Vanzetti's revolver was *not* the one repaired at Iver Johnson's than that it *was* but that Assistant District Attorney Williams had discouraged him from giving this opinion. "Of course, every revolver has a serial number," he testified, "but there was no record of this serial number in court. There was nobody had the number in their possession; nobody knew it, and for that reason that pistol had just a very slim chance that that is the one."[12]

Wadsworth was wrong. The prosecution had the serial number of Berardelli's revolver and knew that it was not Vanzetti's. As Stewart noted in an 18 February memorandum released by the state police in 1977, he had managed to identify the revolver Parmenter had bought when Berardelli went to work for Slater and Morrill.

> Thursday, February 16th, found on the revolver book of
> C. A. Noyes Hardware Company in Brockton a entry showing
> that on October 10, 1919 F. A. Parmenter purchased a Harrington
> and Richardson, 32 calibre, nickel finish, centre fire revolver
> No. 394717.
>
> This revolver was sold to Mr. Parmenter by Karl Tehurnert, a
> salesman in the employ of the above concern.
>
> Went through all the books showing sale of revolvers at this
> concern, which dates from July 10, 1911 to the present day. Was
> told by Mr. Chandler that July 10, 1911 was the day on which they
> sold their first gun.

The revolver Parmenter purchased on 10 October 1919 was not Vanzetti's; it was a .32, not a .38, and the serial number on Vanzetti's gun was G-82581.[13] But it was quite certainly Berardelli's. The date of Parmenter's purchase—October 1919, or six months before the robbery—matches the time at which Mrs. Berardelli said that her husband had been permanently hired by Slater and Morrill. It also matches a date given Officer Brouillard by Edgar M. Beane, an engineer at the Slater and Morrill factory, who in February 1921 said that Parmenter had at one time been in the habit of leaving a gun in the engine room but that that gun had disappeared "about a year and a half ago"—in other words, in September or October 1919.[14] When Parmenter bought a new gun he gave it to Berardelli. Thus, after the shooting Parmenter had told the doctor he had not been armed, while adding that he believed Berardelli was.

In all probability Stewart knew that Parmenter had bought Berardelli's gun at C. A. Noyes even before he went there; otherwise he would not have known where to look. His long search through the records to find another sale of a .38, serial number G-82581, was fruitless. As Thomas Fraher had suspected and as George Fitzmeyer had noted in his repair book, Berardelli's revolver was a .32. Where it was on the day of the robbery no one will ever know, but evidence suggests that Berardelli did not have it with him. At the trial Aldeah Florence, a friend of Mrs. Berardelli, testified that three or four days after the funeral Mrs. Berardelli had said, "Oh dear, if he had taken my advice and taken the revolver out of the shop he would not be, maybe he would not be in the same condition he is today."[15] In any event, the prosecution had discovered that Vanzetti's revolver could not possibly have been Berardelli's. But rather than give up the only piece of physical evidence against Vanzetti, the prosecution successfully concealed their knowledge from the defense and ultimately from the Lowell Committee. Stewart's memorandum sat unnoticed in state police files until 1977.

Furthermore, knowing that the defense might discover the evidence that would disprove the prosecution's claim, Williams waited as long as possible to make it. Williams did not mention the theory in his opening statement. On the seventh day of the trial he began asking Slater and Morrill employee Margaret Mahoney questions about Berardelli's revolver but refused to disclose their purpose when Jerry McAnarney and Judge Thayer questioned their relevance. A similar exchange occurred again the next day during Bostock's testimony, and Thayer insisted that Williams explain himself in a conference at the bench after the assistant district attorney tried to escape by saying, "I think it will be material as the trial progresses."[16] The strategy was rewarded when the defense failed to attack the story head on, merely producing a firearms expert who denied that Vanzetti's revolver had a new hammer.

Today the prosecution's failure to produce this vital piece of exculpatory material would be virtually automatic grounds for a mistrial with respect to Vanzetti. Now that Stewart's memorandum has been produced it will be impossible for anyone to argue Vanzetti's guilt based on his possession of a .38 Harrington and Richardson with a new hammer. The entire case against Vanzetti now rests on the testimony of four eyewitnesses, all of whom, as we have seen, told highly questionable stories. The memorandum is equally significant, however, with respect to what it says about the character of the prosecution. Years later, Williams, then a judge, called Herbert Ehrmann into his chambers to say that while he knew Ehrmann sincerely believed in Sacco and Vanzetti's innocence, he, Williams, believed equally sincerely in their guilt. Katzmann clearly shared this belief. Unfortunately, the prosecution's staff's certainty seems to have made them only too willing to use evidence they knew to be questionable and suppress evidence they knew to be exculpatory. The prosecution's claims with respect to Berardelli's revolver, like their handling of the shotgun shells introduced in the Plymouth trial, their development of the identification testimony, Stewart's "loss" of the paper on which Frank Harding had written the license number of the Bridgewater getaway car, the changes in the police officers' testimony with respect to Sacco and Vanzetti's arrest, and Katzmann's misrepresentation of the defendants' statements on 6 May, convict the prosecution of judicial misconduct. They also entitle us to ask whether they did not tamper with evidence in even more serious ways as well.

9 / Bullet III

hree pieces of physical evidence were introduced against Sacco; two can be dealt with relatively quickly. First, the prosecution introduced a cap. Fred Loring, a Slater and Morrill employee, testified at the trial that he had found a cap lying near Berardelli's body immediately after the shooting; he identified the cap as one introduced at the trial. Sacco's employer, George Kelley, said that the cap in evidence was similar in color to one Sacco had customarily worn, and the prosecution argued that a tear in the lining had occurred when Sacco hung his cap on a nail at work.[1] Kelley is one witness who altered his testimony in a sense favorable to the defense. In an interview with Stewart earlier in June 1921—a full year, it should be noted, after Sacco's arrest—he appeared to recognize the cap.[2]

Posttrial testimony, however, stripped the cap of any evidentiary value. Loring had stated at the trial that he had given the cap to Thomas Fraher, the Slater and Morrill superintendent. Fraher was called to the stand two days later, but the prosecution did not ask him to confirm Loring's story. In December 1921 several Slater and Morrill employees told a defense investigator that Loring had said that he did *not* find the cap.[3] Six years later Jerome Gallivan, the recently retired police chief of Braintree, told the Lowell Committee that Fraher, on 17 April—two days after the crime—had given him a cap that an employee had found on the ground *the previous night*. Subsequently the defense found an item in the *Boston Herald* of 17 April 1920 that confirmed this exactly. A story datelined 16 April in the *Boston Globe* of 17 April confirms that the cap was found on the sixteenth. Furthermore, Gallivan told the Lowell Committee, he had himself made the tear in the lining while looking for a name or other identifying mark inside the cap.[4] Obviously the cap had no evidentiary value whatever. Literally hundreds of workers had come out of the factories immediately after the crime, and the odds against the cap having belonged to one of the bandits were astronomical. Given that the prosecution knew, or could have found out, the true history of the cap and that they concealed it by failing to ask Fraher about it, the cap stands as yet another piece of evidence of prosecution misconduct.[5]

The second piece of evidence against Sacco relates to the thirty-two bullets introduced at the trial as having been found in Sacco's gun and in his pocket on the night of his arrest. They included sixteen Peters cartridges, three Remington U.M.C., seven U.S., and six Winchesters. The six bullets found in Parmenter's and Berardelli's bodies included one Peters, two U.M.C., and three Winchesters. One of the Winchester bullets taken from Berardelli's body, the fatal bullet III, was of a type that had not been manufactured since 1917; two other Winchesters taken from the two bodies were of a more recent type.[6] Bullet III was the bullet claimed to have been fired from Sacco's gun.

The prosecution did not suggest during the trial that Sacco's possession of these particular types of bullet had any significance. When, however, Katzmann was cross-examining James Burns, the defense expert who organized the firearms tests made during the trial, he brought out that Burns and the other experts had not used any Winchester bullets of the type of bullet III during their tests and asked why. Burns replied that Winchester no longer manufactured these bullets. Making a characteristic attempt to discredit the witness, Katzmann asked whether Burns had tried to find any. "Only all through New England here," Burns replied. "That is as far as I could go, between here and Lowell, and around with an automobile, in the time that I had."[7]

Years after the case, a juror indicated that the jury discovered while deliberating that Sacco's six Winchester bullets were of the same pre-1917 type as bullet III, a coincidence that made a deep impression.[8] The Lowell Committee alluded to the same circumstance in its report on the case.[9] The significance of this coincidence was much exaggerated. Burns's response to Katzmann's question suggests that he had looked for bullets of this type in a few stores between Dedham, where he had been staying and observing the trial, and Lowell, where the tests were conducted. He probably stopped once or twice while driving up to do the tests. Neither he nor the other three prosecution and defense experts seem to have thought that it was very important to have such bullets. The difficulty of obtaining the older type of bullet has also been exaggerated by several authors. A defense expert, Albert Hamilton, obtained several in 1923, and a firearms expert consulted by Herbert Ehrmann, one Shelley Braverman, found some as late as 1962! Sacco's own possession of them was perfectly logical. Winchester had discontinued them in 1917, but all its production during 1917 and 1918 had been for war purposes. Sacco said that he had bought a mixed box of cartridges in either 1917 or 1918, when these would still have been the only Winchesters available.[10]

Nor is the commonality of the types of bullets taken from the murdered men's bodies and Sacco's bullets as impressive as it seems. Both sets of bullets included bullets of U.M.C. and Peters make, as well as the obsolete Winchester type. But Sacco's bullets also included U.S. cartridges, none of which were found on the bodies, while the murder bullets included two more recent Winchester bullets, which Sacco did not possess. The significance of the bullets is further lessened since all these were extremely common types of bullets and since the prosecution never claimed that Sacco's gun had fired any but the one obsolete Winchester anyway.

Much more serious, however, was the firearms evidence against Sacco—the only prosecution evidence that has grown stronger, not weaker, since the trial. We have seen that four bullets had been taken from Berardelli's body and two from Parmenter's. James Bostock, an eyewitness to the shooting, said at the trial that he had found "three or four" empty shells near the two bodies. At the trial two expert prosecution witnesses—Captain Proctor and Charles Van Amburgh—gave opinions of varying but not complete certainty that *one* of the bullets taken from Berardelli's body, known as bullet III, had been fired through the Colt.32 automatic found on Sacco on the night of his arrest. Van Amburgh also said that there was a "very strong similarity" between *one* of the "Fraher shells" (so called because Superintendent Fraher gave them to Captain Proctor), a Winchester known as shell w, and test shells fired from Sacco's pistol. Two defense experts argued that neither the bullet nor the shell had come from Sacco's Colt. We shall see that Captain Proctor later swore an affidavit indicating that his trial testimony was only meant to indicate that bullet III had been fired from the same *type* of pistol as Sacco's Colt. By modern standards none of these opinions was worth very much. The comparison microscope, which enables experts to make such judgments with a high degree of certainty, had not yet been developed, and forensic ballistics as practiced in 1921 was far from an exact science.

In 1927 Major Calvin Goddard, a pioneer in the use of the comparison microscope, made an informal examination of bullet III, shell w, and bullets and shells test-fired from Sacco's gun. He concluded that bullet III and shell w both had been fired from Sacco's Colt. In the same year, William G. Thompson, who had taken over Sacco and Vanzetti's defense in 1923, argued that the prosecution had fraudulently substituted bullet III for an original bullet. The defense tried to buttress this claim scientifically. Dr. George Magrath, who removed the bullets from Berardelli's body, testified at the trial that he had marked them seriatim with scratches from a surgical needle. Several firearms experts and attorneys who examined the bullets in 1927 noticed that the markings on the base of bullet III differed so much from those on the other bullets that they appeared to have been made by a different instrument.[11] A defense expert, Wilbur Turner, told the Lowell Committee that there was "a tremendous difference in the marking, as though they were made with a different tool or scratched with a different instrument." President Lowell implicitly acknowledged this by suggesting that Dr. Magrath might have marked bullet III with a different instrument.[12] Lieutenant John Collins of the Massachusetts State Police noted the difference in the markings in 1961.[13]

In 1961 Francis Russell arranged for two new experts, Frank Jury and Jac Weller, to make new tests. Using a comparison microscope, they also concluded that bullet III and shell W must have come from Sacco's Colt. They also concluded, as had all the earlier experts, that the other three bullets removed from Berardelli's body and the two taken from Parmenter's had been fired from a single unknown weapon, as had the other three Fraher shells. Grounds exist for questioning the results of both the Goddard (1927) and the Jury and Weller (1961) tests. Goddard, despite his comparison microscope, had to admit error in a subsequent murder case. Jury and Weller, it turned out, had previously published their opinion that bullet III had been fired from Sacco's pistol, and Weller had also made a critical error in a murder case some years earlier.[14] Furthermore, in requesting permission to make the tests Russell wrote the Department of Public Safety that he expected them to show that Sacco's pistol had fired bullet III, and Weller wrote a state police officer that he would not want to criticize American justice or any individual police department.[15]

In 1983, in the course of producing a documentary on the case, a Boston television station, WBZ, commissioned a panel of distinguished forensic firearms experts to examine the evidence again. The panel made a very thorough examination of the evidence and apparently settled some of the most important issues once and for all. After test-firing Sacco's pistol once again and cleaning bullet III, they determined that both bullet III and shell W had indeed been fired from Sacco's pistol. They also found that the other five bullets and the other three shells had been fired from the same pistol, and tentatively identified that pistol as a Harrington and Richardson .32 automatic—a finding which, as we shall see, blasts the most popular prosecution and defense theories of the case out of the water. The panel also found that some of the Peters cartridges found upon Sacco at the time of his arrest had been made by the same machine as the two Peters shells found at the scene of the crime. Without a great deal more data concerning the manufacturing procedures of the Peters company, however, the significance of this finding is impossible to evaluate.[16]

Despite the problems surrounding the 1927 and 1961 tests, then, the 1983 examination seems definitely to have established that the bullet III introduced in the trial probably did come from Sacco's pistol. The results of these tests do not, however, establish Sacco's guilt or complicity in the South Braintree murders. Virtually conclusive evidence shows that bullet III and shell w were not genuine exhibits but were test-fired by the prosecution sometime during the year between the arrest and the trial of Sacco and Vanzetti. Much of this evidence is not new; it is almost as old as the crime itself. It comes from the testimony of the eyewitnesses to the crime and the trial testimony of Drs. George Magrath, Frederick Jones, and John Frazer, who performed the autopsies on Parmenter and Berardelli. Read carefully, this evidence virtually rules out the possibility that bullet III was fired from a different weapon than the other five murder bullets—either from Sacco's Colt or from another .32 caliber Colt automatic. It leads instead to the conclusion that all these bullets were fired from the same weapon—and that bullet III, in particular, could not have been fired from a different gun.

The puzzle of the bullets can be solved by reconstructing the actual shooting with the help of the eyewitness testimony and the testimony of the autopsy surgeons. The eyewitness testimony must be approached with caution; it shows the same problems previously noted with respect to identification testimony. The murder of Parmenter and Berardelli took place in broad daylight in full view of numerous onlookers, but it was a quick and frightening event that generated contradictory eyewitness accounts. Many witnesses gave wild and fragmentary accounts of what they had seen; many in particular fell into the common error of exaggerating the number of shots, bandits, guns, and even automobiles that had been involved in the crime itself. Fortunately, three well-placed witnesses gave calm, coherent, and above all consistent accounts of the shooting within a few days after it took place. What is more significant is that the most important parts of their testimony are corroborated by the more reliable evidence of the autopsy surgeons.

As figure 11 shows, Parmenter and Berardelli were attacked as they walked eastward along the south side of Pearl Street, just as they passed the Rice and Hutchins factory on their right. The two men who attacked

11. The scene of the crime, looking west along Pearl Street.
The Rice and Hutchins factory is on the left. The bandits waited by the
fence in front of the factory until Parmenter and Berardelli walked
by them. Bostock watched the shooting from directly in front of the
water tank across the street; McGlone was on the same side of the street
as Bostock but slightly further east. Wade was out of the picture on
the same side of the street as the bandits but well to the east.
(Courtesy Massachusetts Supreme Judicial Court)

them had been leaning for some time against the fence next to the sidewalk by the corner of the factory; the car that took them away had been waiting perhaps a hundred yards farther down Pearl Street, which sloped downward from west to east—that is, in the direction Parmenter and Berardelli were walking. The three witnesses with the best view of the shooting were Lewis Wade, an employee of Slater and Morrill, who stood roughly two hundred feet down the grade from Parmenter and Berardelli, on the same side of the street; James McGlone, a teamster, who was standing almost directly across Pearl Street from where the shooting took place; and James Bostock, a machinist, who had just passed Parmenter and Berardelli as he walked in the other direction and saw the shooting from about fifty feet away, on the other side of the street and to the west. Wade was in front of Parmenter and Berardelli; Bostock was slightly behind them; and McGlone was immediately on their left.

Wade and McGlone gave by far the most detailed and coherent accounts of the shooting at the inquest two days after the crime at Quincy District Court on 17 April 1920, and while Bostock was not called at the inquest he told his story to a Pinkerton operative on 22 April. At that time Bostock also reported that Parmenter, who did not die until the night of the shooting, had said that the two bandits loitering by the fence had allowed Parmenter and Berardelli, who were walking side by side with Berardelli on the right, to walk past them before starting to shoot. Thus the first few shots, which most of the witnesses did not see, were fired from behind the two guards, a fact confirmed by autopsy evidence.[17]

Lewis Wade, standing by the Slater and Morrill factory down the street from the shooting, thought he looked up after the first shot, and he apparently did see more of the action than McGlone or Bostock. "I saw Berardelli and Parmenter," he said at the inquest.

> I stood there and after the first shot Berardelli sank to the ground. We thought the second time they got Parmenter, he started to run across the road with the boxes. . . . [Berardelli was standing] with his arm up like that. A young fellow . . . bare headed, in a crouching position and kind of stooped over, was there. I didn't know but what he was looking for his hat. Two fellows went across the road after Parmenter, leaving this Italian alone with Berardelli. As he stood over him he took a gun and shot twice. Before that Berardelli's arm was moving and I thought reaching for his gun, and

after the two shots were over Berardelli lay very still with his arm out.

We shall see that one of these shots was bullet III, which took a downward course through Berardelli's body. After he fired these shots the bandit raised his hand, and the car came up the hill; the bandits picked up the money boxes and jumped in. Wade noticed the bandit's determination to kill Berardelli rather than simply to disable him and concluded that Berardelli had known his assailant. He also saw a shot fired from the car as it drove away.[18]

At the trial Wade gave more detailed testimony.

> As I turned there and looked up the road, I saw Parmenter run, and as he ran across the road he ran like that (*illustrating*) and . . .
> I couldn't see him no more. I looked at Berardelli, and he was in a crouching position. That means his left arm was up here, and he was down like that. And this man was standing, well, not at the most over five feet, anyway, from him, and he was in a crouching position. He was over like that, jumping back and forth, and I saw him shoot. Then I saw him shoot again.
> Q. In what direction? A. Towards the man on the sidewalk, Berardelli. That would be, shooting south. Berardelli stood in an angle on north-east, and the man that was shooting him was facing south. [It was not by an amazing feat of memory that Wade recalled the directions involved; he had a map in front of him while giving his testimony.]

This makes clear that the bandit who stood over Berardelli and fired into him fired from the front. Wade added that Berardelli "dropped on to his left side and rolled over onto his back."[19]

At the inquest McGlone, who was standing directly across the street helping to excavate for a new building, testified that he had looked up after the first shot or two. "I saw one fellow have hold of the guard [Berardelli] and when I looked over two shots were fired at him," he said. "After I looked over there were two men right there. He had hold of the guard and put two shots into him. Q. How did he hold him? A. He held his shoulder with his left hand and the pistol in his right." He added that the pistol was no more than eight or nine inches from the guard and that after the two shots "the guard dropped." At that moment

Parmenter came across the street, almost directly at him, and collapsed. Not having seen Parmenter shot, he concluded that he had already been shot, before Berardelli. Several times he repeated that Berardelli had been shot twice, then collapsed. He had seen two other bandits, but—a significant and generally overlooked point—he said that neither of them had a gun. A car came up the hill, and the bandits seized the money boxes containing the payroll and jumped into it. As it drove away one bandit fired a shot from the running board at Berardelli lying on the ground.[20] McGlone told virtually the same story at the trial.[21]

Bostock had passed the two payroll guards as he walked west on Pearl Street; as he told the Pinkerton operative, he turned around after hearing shots. "Turning around he [Bostock] saw Beredelli [sic] crouched on the ground with his left arm shielding his face and one of the men he had seen loitering was standing within three feet of Beredelli shooting into Beredelli's body. The other man he had seen loitering was shooting at Parmenter and after Parmenter had dropped the box, containing the money, the bandit fired twice more into Parmenter's back." Then the car came up the hill and stopped, and the driver, he said, got out to help pick up the money boxes.[22] Bostock amplified his testimony slightly at the trial: "As I looked down there, this Berardelli was on his knees in a crouched position as though he were guarding with his hand over his head, as though he was guarding himself, and this man stood off. . . . he stood there over him. He shot, I should say, he shot at Berardelli probably four or five times. He stood guard over him." The bandit then fired twice toward Bostock himself and seemed to refill his gun. He repeated that he had seen another bandit shooting Parmenter twice while Parmenter was coming across the street.[23] We shall find that Bostock's testimony cannot have been completely accurate, but he corroborated the critical detail of a bandit standing over Berardelli and shooting him several times.

The detailed trial testimony of three autopsy surgeons—Drs. Jones, Frazer, and Magrath—regarding the wounds that Berardelli and Parmenter received enables us to determine when bullet iii was fired and whether it could actually have been fired from a different weapon than the others.[24] Parmenter was hit by two bullets. The bullet that killed him entered his body in the right side of the lower back, just below his twelfth and last rib, and traversed his body from right to left, severing the vena cava and lodging in the front of his abdomen slightly on the left side of his body. The second bullet struck him in the chest just below the tip of his breastbone. Apparently fired from his right, it barely penetrated his body and traveled just a few inches to the left, exiting his body just below his left nipple.[25]

Berardelli was hit by four bullets, which Dr. Magrath marked I through IV with Roman numerals as he removed them from the guard's body (actually, the fourth bullet was marked IIII). Bullet I had struck him on the left side of his back, about six inches to the left of his spine and two inches below his armpit, and traveled to the left and somewhat downward, encircling his chest cavity and coming to rest at the front of the left chest. Bullet II had struck him at the rear of his upper left arm, four inches from the top of his shoulder and an inch and a half from the armpit side of the arm. Going into his arm, it had passed through his shoulder and continued through his pectoral muscle, traversing his chest between the second and third ribs and coming to rest under his third rib on the right side of his body. Bullet III had hit him on the right side of his upper back, near his right shoulder, about six inches to the right of his spine and three inches from the top of the shoulder. It had gone through his torso diagonally downward and from right to left, passing through his right lung, through the aorta, through his left kidney, and finally lodging against his left hip. It is immediately obvious that this bullet, which Dr. Magrath identified as the one that killed him, was fired by someone standing over a crouching or kneeling Berardelli, since it traveled almost straight downward through his body. By passing through the aorta this bullet killed him almost instantly. Finally, bullet IV had struck Berardelli in the lower left back, about six inches from his spine and an inch and a half below the crest of his hip bone. Going through his hip, it had traveled on a diagonal from left to right across his body and slightly upward, coming to rest in the right abdomen. The numbered sequence of the bullets was not designed in any way to reflect the order in which they had struck Berardelli but merely showed the order in which Dr. Magrath had removed them from his body.[26]

Once again it is essential to note that several firearms tests have shown that the two bullets that struck Parmenter and bullets I, II, and IV taken from Berardelli's body all came from the same automatic, as did three of the four shells introduced by the prosecution as having been found at the scene of the crime. The critical question with respect to the possibility of a substitution of bullet III and shell W by the prosecution is whether the eyewitness testimony and autopsy reports allow for the possibility that bullet III was fired by a different weapon than the others.

The answer is that the evidence virtually rules out this possibility.

The tracks of the bullets confirm Parmenter's statement that a bandit began firing at Parmenter and Berardelli from behind, after the two men had passed the bandits by the fence. He hit Berardelli in the lower left back with bullet IV, which traveled from left to right and slightly upward. The bullet traveled upward because Berardelli was walking downhill, and was probably bent over slightly owing to the weight of the payroll. He also seems to have hit Parmenter with the shot that struck him in the back, traversed his body from right to left, and eventually killed him. Both men then seem to have turned toward the man firing at them. Parmenter turned to his right and was struck by the bullet that entered his chest at the tip of his breastbone and exited under his left nipple. Berardelli apparently turned to his left, exposing the left side of his body in a way that enabled him to receive the wound in the back of his left arm, which shot across his chest (bullet II). He then sank to the ground. As Parmenter began running across the road, another bandit chased him across the road to get his money box. Bostock thought that this man was firing at Parmenter, but he was mistaken. McGlone, directly across from Parmenter, realized that he had been shot well before he got across the road and noticed that the man who actually chased him across the road to get his payroll box did not have a gun.

The gunman now stepped up to Berardelli. By this time all three witnesses were looking directly at the gunman, and while their descriptions of what follows vary slightly they are complementary rather than contradictory. McGlone saw the gunman holding Berardelli with his left hand, firing two shots into him. Bostock saw Berardelli raising his left arm as the gunman stood over him and fired "four or five times"; he evidently exaggerated the number of shots in a manner characteristic of eyewitnesses. Wade saw Berardelli crouching "with his arm up"; the bandit stood over him "jumping back and forth," shot him twice, and Berardelli fell on his left side and rolled over on his back. Wade's testimony that the gunman was facing south while Berardelli was facing northeast indicates clearly that the bandit was standing in front of the guard. Bostock evidently exaggerated the number of shots; other than that, the testimony of all three men is remarkably consistent. The bandit stood over Berardelli and fired at least two shots at point-blank range.[27]

Bullet III, which struck Berardelli behind his right shoulder and traveled downward and from right to left through his body, was obviously one of the shots that Wade, McGlone, and Bostock saw a bandit fire downward at Berardelli as he crouched on the ground. *The bullet III introduced in evidence can only be genuine if the bandit who fired it did not hit Berardelli with any other shots.* But the eyewitnesses agree that *one* bandit, with *one* gun, stood over Berardelli and fired *two* shots at him. Their testimony in itself would not be conclusive. It is conceivable that all three might have succumbed to the common tendency toward exaggeration and seen two shots when only one was actually fired. Also, the gunman might simply have missed once, although he was so close to Berardelli that this seems highly unlikely. But the autopsy evidence confirms that the gunman standing over Berardelli hit him with two shots and therefore tends to prove that the bullet III introduced in evidence cannot be genuine.

Dr. Magrath's testimony clearly indicates that *two* bullets traveled downward and from right to left through Berardelli's body. One of them, of course, was the fatal bullet III, which struck him on the back below his right shoulder and traveled downward and to the left, severing his aorta and lodging against his left hip. The other was bullet I, which struck him on the upper left back and whose track Dr. Magrath discussed in response to a question from the assistant district attorney, Harold Williams, on 8 June 1920.

What I have in mind, the course taken by the bullet which made wound No. II [this was bullet I; see *The Sacco-Vanzetti Case*, 1:115] in the left side of the back—and circular, tending to circle the chest—may have taken the course which it did because it did not strike the surface of the body at right angles. The skin around that wound above it and toward the middle line is somewhat bruised, *as would be the case if that bullet struck the skin at an oblique angle and if the bullet was pointing somewhat downward and to the left* [emphasis added], instead of going straight at the back. This condition of the skin suggests an oblique and not a right angle of impact on the part of the bullet. The fact that it did not penetrate the chest directly, did not penetrate it at any time, but circled around it, also leads to the opinion that it may not have struck at a right angle. The bullet, being of the kind which tends to keep right straight on, being a jacketed bullet of much penetrating power, it may have been expected that a bullet striking squarely would keep on going. In this instance the bullet circled around the chest in the muscles and soft parts. . . . That is, the line of flight of the bullet towards the body, instead of being straight at the back where the hole was, may have been somewhat downward and to the left and from slightly above.[28]

Although bullets I and III struck Berardelli on different parts of his back, both traveled downward and from right to left. They traveled downward because, as all three witnesses testified, the bandit stood over a crouching Berardelli when he fired them; they traveled from right to left because the bandit was standing not directly in front of him but on a slight diagonal to Berardelli's right. This is confirmed by Wade's testimony that Berardelli was facing northeast and the bandit was facing south. The downward track of bullet III is more pronounced than that of bullet I because Berardelli was trying to rise and had evidently lifted his torso to a slightly more erect position when bullet III struck him. At the grand jury proceeding Wade gave testimony that would explain this perfectly: "The first shot [Berardelli] crumpled up and the second shot he crumpled up further and the last shot he went to the ground." Then Berardelli collapsed onto his left side and rolled over onto his back.[29]

Thus, the same bandit and the same gun fired bullets I and III. And since firearms tests have matched bullet I to the four remaining bullets, it is clear that all the shots that struck the two men were fired by one bandit, who was designated by his cohorts to disable or kill the guards while the others picked up the payroll boxes. This ties in with the evidence of McGlone, who stated at the inquest that he saw only one man with a revolver. A bandit did fire a further shot at Berardelli from the running board of the getaway car as it moved up the hill away from the scene, but by this time Berardelli had fallen onto his left side and onto his back with his head facing in the direction the car was going —positions in which a shot from the car could not possibly have hit him where bullet III did, even making allowances for extraordinary marksmanship.

Additional evidence also helps rule out the possibility of bullet III's having been fired from a different gun. At the trial Bostock, in another critically important but generally ignored piece of testimony, stated that the bandit who fired down into Berardelli subsequently looked up, fired two shots in the direction of Bostock himself, *and proceeded to reload his gun*.[30] This testimony would make perfect sense if this bandit had fired the six bullets that struck the two guards, plus one or two at Bostock. A .32 caliber automatic of the type that fired the bullets held as many as nine bullets. But it would make no sense at all if the bandit had fired only one shot at Berardelli, or even two, and two in Bostock's direction—unless one believes that the bandit had undertaken this carefully planned robbery with a half-empty gun. When Sacco was arrested his gun was fully loaded with eleven bullets.[31] If he was the man Bostock saw fire bullet III, he reloaded his gun after firing only two or three.

The conclusion that the bullet III introduced by the prosecution was substituted for an original exhibit leads to the conclusion that shell w, which matches it, is not genuine either. There was no need to substitute shell w for a genuine shell, since the shells found on the ground had never been marked for identification.[32]

The three other shells introduced by the prosecution provide additional evidence of a substitution. They included a U.M.C. shell and *two* Peters shells. Only *one* of the six bullets taken from the victims' bodies was identified by expert witnesses as a Peters bullet. The presence of the extra Peters shell could be accounted for in three ways. It could match a bullet fired in the early stages of the attack that missed both guards; in this case it would have no particular significance. It could have come from one of the shots that Bostock saw the bandit who killed Berardelli fire in his own direction after shooting the guard; since both Peters shells were fired from a Harrington and Richardson automatic and since the bandit who fired toward Bostock was the same bandit who fired bullet III into Berardelli as he crouched on the ground, this would also confirm that bullet III was a substitute. Finally, this shell could be the one that matched the original bullet III.

The eyewitness testimony and the autopsy reports indicate that the bullet III introduced at the trial and tested in 1927 and 1961 did not come from Berardelli's body and that shell w was not found on the ground on the day of the crime. They do not, however, tell the whole story. Other new evidence indicates when, how, and why the substitution took place.

10 / How the Frame Occurred

New documentation provides substantial confirmation for the theory that bullet III and shell w were not genuine exhibits but were substituted by the prosecution. Available evidence indicates that the four bullets originally taken from Berardelli's body—as well as the two taken from Parmenter's—were actually fired from the same weapon and that only three rather than four shells were originally found on the ground near Berardelli's body. The minutes of the trial show how District Attorney Williams took careful precautions to make sure that the substitution of a new bullet III was not discovered. There is no exact proof, and there almost certainly never can be, of exactly how, when, and by whom a switch was made, but there is enough evidence to allow for reasonable answers to these questions.

The problem of determining whether the original bullets were indeed fired from the same gun and did *not* include a bullet fired from a Colt automatic is somewhat simpler than a layman might think. While the six rifling marks on bullet III all slant to the left, the rifling marks on the other bullets—oval gouges extending more than halfway up the bullet—slant to the right. As figure 12 shows, the difference in the markings on bullet III could be noticed by anyone who looked at the bullets closely and would certainly be noticed immediately by anyone with any knowledge of firearms evidence. It was the left twist that immediately marked bullet III as having come from a Colt automatic such as Sacco's.[1] In fact, evidence that has long been in the public record tends to support the theory that the four bullets originally taken from Berardelli's body were similar in appearance. "There were two bullets that entered the body of Parmenter and four entered the body of Berardelli," Dr. Jones said at the inquest on 17 April. "I have seen all those bullets and they are all identical, all 32 calibre, short automatic, jacketed. . . . If one were to deduce from the wounds and from the bullets they were all fired by the same type of pistol and easily carried in a pocket automatic pistol." However, Dr. Jones quickly added that he was "no expert" regarding bullets and that he had not examined the Berardelli bullets very carefully.[2] The grand jury proceeding—unknown until now—provides more definite information.

Dr. George Magrath, who removed the bullets from Berardelli's body, testified before the grand jury at some length on 10 September 1920. His

12. The four bullets introduced at the trial as having come from Berardelli's body. Note the leftward slant of the grooves on bullet III, *third from left*, and the rightward slant of the grooves on the other bullets. (Courtesy Jet Commercial Photographers, Boston)

answers to Katzmann's questions regarding the bullets must be quoted in full.

> Q. In plain English, he [Berardelli] was shot from behind? A. He was shot from behind, three of the wounds from his left side to his hip to a fourth from behind toward the middle of the body and diagonally backward. These four bullets I placed in the hands of Captain Proctor on August 3rd at his office in the State House. The bullets are all alike; they were jacketed and weighed 4 and 1/10 grammes; the dimensions and weight are consistent with what is known as a .32 caliber made to be used in an automatic pistol.

>   .   .   .   .   .

> Q. In your opinion were those bullets all fired by the same gun? A. I have an opinion that they all may have been fired by the same gun, but I have no proof. The bullets were all of the same size and weight. A final determination I did not make, but I have a belief that they were fired from the same weapon and they very well could have been, judging from the size and weight.
> Q. They were the same type of bullet? A. *They looked exactly alike* [emphasis added].

>   .   .   .   .   .

> Q. [After a discussion of Parmenter's wounds and the bullet removed from his body] What was the caliber of it [the Parmenter bullet]? A. It was a jacketed bullet 7 mm. in diameter,—the

same size and character as the bullets previously removed from
the body of Baradelli [*sic*], .32, of the kind used in an automatic
pistol.

Q. *You have personally been in consultation with me on experiments as to the type of gun from which the four bullets were discharged? You did not personally experiment to see?* A. No, I did not [emphasis added].[3]

As the medical examiner of populous Suffolk County, which includes Boston, Dr. Magrath removed dozens if not hundreds of bullets from bodies every year. He testified in numerous criminal cases. A pioneer in legal medicine, he was keenly interested in forensic science.[4] He may easily have had some knowledge of the ways by which bullets could be matched to the weapons that fired them, and if he did, he would have noticed any difference in the rifling marks at once. In addition, it *is* clear from the testimony that he had looked at the bullets carefully, and he did say that they looked "exactly alike." Magrath's testimony, while inconclusive, tends to indicate that the original Berardelli bullets did not include one with a left twist and that a switch subsequently took place.[5]

More significantly, it is clear from the grand jury minutes that Magrath's opinion was not the only one that Katzmann had. At the time Magrath testified, the four Berardelli bullets had been in Captain Proctor's possession for more than five weeks. Proctor's knowledge of firearms was such that he would have immediately noticed if one of the bullets had a left twist that marked it as having been fired from a Colt automatic. Katzmann's statement to Magrath—"You have personally been in consultation with me on experiments as to the type of gun from which the four bullets were discharged?"—clearly indicates that someone, almost surely Proctor, had been looking into this question. Yet, both in this statement and in his earlier question regarding Magrath's own opinion, *Katzmann's choice of words indicates that he shared the opinion that all the bullets had come from the same gun.* Furthermore, if Proctor had told Katzmann that one bullet had come from a Colt like Sacco's, this would have been an important piece of evidence to put before the grand jury—but Katzmann did not even call Proctor to the stand or identify Sacco's gun as a Colt. While barely short of being conclusive proof, the grand jury testimony strongly indicates that as of September 1920 the bullets did not include one fired from a Colt.

New evidence regarding the shells found near Berardelli's body is much more specific. The prosecution at the trial introduced four shells, which James Bostock, the machinist and eyewitness to the crime, claimed to have found near Berardelli's body. But Bostock's testimony is contradicted by a handwritten summary of the evidence in a notebook belonging to Assistant District Attorney Harold Williams, a notebook that seems to date from January or February 1921. The notebook includes the statement, "Shay picked up 3 shells where Ber fell and gave them to Sherlock."[6] John Shay was a police officer who in February 1921 was helping to investigate the case. A subsequent typewritten outline repeated that Shay had found the shells but added that he had given them to Thomas Fraher, the Slater and Morrill superintendent. This is doubly significant since it suggests that Williams had checked his information, discovering that Shay had actually given the shells to Fraher rather than to Sherlock but confirming that Shay had found them. (The typewritten notes do not give a number.)

The possibility that Williams was simply mistaken becomes remote in light of other evidence that suggests that Bostock was induced to perjure himself on this point at the trial, presumably because Shay, who did not testify, declined to state that he had found four shells. Bostock had been interviewed by a Pinkerton operative a few days after the crime; he was also interviewed by Officer John Scott in January or February 1921.[7] In both interviews Bostock gave a thorough account of what he had seen; in neither one did he say one word about finding shells. "As soon as the car had passed," he told the Pinkerton operative, "he went to Berardelli and raised him in his arms, but saw that he was dead, so went across the street to Parmenter and helped carry Parmenter into Mrs. Colberts and stayed with Parmenter until he was taken to the hospital."[8] When would he have had time to look for shells? Indeed, Bostock's trial testimony indicates that he had not quite gotten his new story straight. First, he had to be prompted to mention the shells. Williams initially asked him, "Did you see anything near the scene of the shooting when you went down there except the bodies of Berardelli and Parmenter?" and received the reply, "No sir, I did not." Williams then specifically asked whether Bostock had picked up shells and got an affirmative reply. Second, Bostock said not that he had picked up four shells but that he had picked up "three or four." Third, while Bostock said that he had left them in a desk in Slater and Morrill's and denied that he had given them to superintendent Thomas Fraher, Fraher testified that Bostock had given them to him personally.[9] This was not the only instance in which Bostock proved a pliable witness. We have seen how Williams induced him to say that he had seen Berardelli with his revolver on the Saturday night before the shooting, only to have Bostock admit on cross-examination that he had not actually seen the revolver at that time. Bostock was also one of the few witnesses who refused before the trial to talk to defense investigators.[10]

Other trial testimony suggests that the prosecution desperately feared that the substitution of bullet III might be discovered. In his opening statement, Harold Williams stated that the prosecution would show that the mortal bullet III had been fired by a Colt automatic such as had been carried by Sacco.[11] Williams had to ask Dr. Magrath to identify the bullets, however, and the doctor might conceivably have realized that the new bullet III was not genuine. The trial transcript shows how Williams decided to handle this problem.

On the surface there would seem to have been little risk of Magrath's realizing that the bullet III put into his hand in Dedham Courthouse was not the one he had removed from Berardelli's body over a year earlier. Having removed dozens of bullets from bodies in the intervening months, he could hardly be expected to remember the appearance of any particular one. The difficulty, as Williams knew, was that Magrath believed that all four of the Berardelli bullets had come from the same gun and had said that they looked exactly alike.[12] Magrath might notice either the different appearance of the rifling marks or a difference in the scratches in the base of the substituted bullet III. Williams had to deny Magrath any opportunity to compare bullet III and the other bullets. The transcript of Magrath's testimony shows how cleverly Williams managed this.

> Q. Let me show you these bullets, Doctor, and see if you can identify them as the bullets removed from the body of Berardelli *(handing bullets to the witness)*.
>
> MR. WILLIAMS. May we have a little light, Sheriff?
> *(The sheriff turns on the lights.)*
>
> THE WITNESS. I identify that *(indicating)* as the bullet which I numbered "III" by placing three vertical marks upon it, on the left base.
>
> Q. Is there any objection to me showing this bullet to the jury?
> A. None whatever. I am not sure that light in the jury box will show the light marks. If it doesn't, use the lens.
> [The bullet was offered and shown to the defense.]

Q. What kind of a bullet is that? A. It is a jacketed bullet, of the size consistent with what is known as 32 calibre.

Q. *Can you personally tell, Doctor, from what type of gun or shooting weapon that bullet was fired?* A. *No.* [Emphasis added.]

MR. WILLIAMS *(to the jury)*. Mr. Foreman, just look at that bullet and see if it is flattened in any way and look at the mark on the base. If you cannot see them with this reading glass very likely you can with the smaller glass. If any of you have any difficulty with it, I have a little more powerful glass.

Q. I will ask you, Doctor, *to save possibly a longer examination of other bullets* [emphasis added], if the other marks on the other bullets which you are about to examine are Roman numerals similar in character to that No. III on the bottom of the bullet? A. They are; the number 4 being represented by four vertical lines and not by "I" and a "V," but by four vertical lines.

     .   .   .   .   .   .

Q. Doctor, if you will replace that in the envelope marked "Bullet No. III." Now, if you will examine envelope marked "Bullet No. II" and tell us what you find there. A. This envelope contains a jacketed bullet bearing two marks which I placed upon its base, known as No. "II" of my record.
[Bullet II becomes Exhibit 19.]

MR. WILLIAMS *(showing Exhibit 19 to the jury). Just pass it around to show its general appearance, gentlemen. That is all you need to do, I guess, unless you care to do otherwise* [emphasis added]. [The other bullets were then examined and admitted one by one.][13]

By showing bullet III to Magrath first and by showing him the bullets one by one Williams denied Magrath any opportunity to compare them and to notice the difference either in their rifling marks or in their scratches. By encouraging the jury not to look closely at the scratches in bullets II, I, and IV, he reduced the likelihood of their noticing it either. Finally, knowing that Magrath had told Katzmann before the grand jury that he had not experimented to determine the type of gun from which the bullets had been fired, Williams induced Magrath to put his ignorance on this point on record so that he would be unable to challenge any subsequent testimony. Such a subterfuge would not have been necessary had Magrath merely been mistaken in his grand jury testimony; the prosecution could simply have pointed out his mistake. As it was, Williams took a tremendous gamble and got away with it.

When did the switch take place? It must have taken place between September 1920 and February of 1921. Williams's notebook, which seems to date from late January or early February of 1921, states specifically that the four Berardelli bullets include a bullet fired from a Colt automatic.[14] The switch could have been perpetrated either by Captain Proctor or by Charles Van Amburgh, a second expert whom the prosecution apparently brought into the case because it was dissatisfied with Proctor's opinion about the bullets, or by Chief Stewart and State Police Officer Albert Brouillard, the officers who actually investigated the case. The question of why any of these men would have undertaken such a serious step involves the most extraordinary irony of the entire case. Students of the case have consistently misinterpreted the prosecution's motives because they have misunderstood the state of knowledge of the prosecution's firearms experts. In actual fact, the prosecution does not seem to have realized that a switch would provide seemingly irrefutable proof of Sacco's guilt. The reason is that they did not believe that it was possible to identify the specific weapon from which a bullet or shell had been fired.

As we have seen, grand jury testimony suggests that by September 1920 Katzmann solicited Proctor's opinion regarding the four Berardelli bullets. We do not know for certain what Proctor told him, but we do know for certain, based on posttrial statements by both Proctor and Harold Williams, that the prosecution was dissatisfied with Proctor's opinion and called in Charles Van Amburgh as a result. At the trial Van Amburgh said specifically that he first examined the firearms evidence in the case in December 1920.[15] In the meantime, there is no record of the custody of the bullets between 3 August 1920, when Magrath gave them to Proctor, and the trial. Although Williams asked Proctor during this testimony to confirm his continuous custody of almost all the firearms evidence in the case, *he specifically omitted any such question relating to the four Berardelli bullets.*[16] The only other piece of evidence for which he also omitted such a question was Vanzetti's revolver, which, as we have seen, Stewart had in his possession for several weeks. Proctor evidently refused to testify as to his custody of the bullets. There is, indeed, a suspicious lack of material relating to the firearms evidence against Sacco either in the state police files or in the prosecution's papers at the Harvard Law School Library. While these papers document fairly well the prosecution's search for eyewitness testimony and give a good account of Stewart's attempts to identify Vanzetti's revolver, they contain nothing regarding Proctor's or Van Amburgh's pretrial investigations of the bullets.

In the authors' opinion, the switch was probably perpetrated by Stewart and Brouillard sometime before Van Amburgh's examination in December 1920. The two men presumably test-fired Sacco's gun, substituted the resulting bullet for the original bullet III, and added the resulting shell to the three original shells at that time. They must have selected bullet III not because it was the mortal bullet—something which at that time they would probably not have known—but because the bullet they fired became flattened during the test and because bullet III was the only bullet that had a flattened appearance.[17] The prosecution did not have to substitute shell w because none of the original shells had been marked.

Curiously, even after Van Amburgh's examination, the prosecution obviously did not regard bullet III as decisive evidence against Sacco. Even in his opening statement at the trial Williams said only that the prosecution would show that bullet III and shell w had been fired from the type of weapon carried by Sacco and not by his particular weapon. This has been advanced as evidence that no switch had taken place, but this conclusion is erroneous. The reason for the prosecution's reticence was simply that neither Proctor nor Van Amburgh believed in 1921 that a bullet could be matched to a particular weapon with any real certainty.

Captain William Proctor was the senior officer of the Massachusetts State Police and, apparently, the ranking forensic firearms expert in Massachusetts at the time of the South Braintree murders. Over the previous twenty years he had given firearms evidence in more than one hundred capital cases.[18] Yet, while he believed that it was possible by comparing bullets to determine *the type of gun from which particular bullets or shells had been fired*, he did not believe that it was possible to match bullets *to any particular gun*. This emerges, in the first instance, from an excerpt from his testimony in another 1915 case, submitted as evidence to the Lowell Committee in 1927.

> Q. (*by District Attorney Sullivan*) Having examined the double cuts which you have described in the bullets which you received from Dr. Foster, and having examined the double cut in the bullets which you forced through this revolver, Exhibit 10,

did you come to any probable conclusion as to the revolver
from which these two bullets that you got from Dr. Foster were
fired? A. I come to the conclusion that *it was consistent—*
those two bullets,—with having been fired from this revolver
or a revolver that had an imperfection exactly like it [emphasis
added].[19]

In his Dedham testimony in 1921 Proctor confirmed that his tech-
nique was to push bullets through revolvers and measure the grooves, or
rifling marks, upon them so as to determine the characteristic markings
left by particular types of revolvers, and that he pushed bullets through
suspected murder weapons to provide bullets that could be compared
with those removed from the victim's body. This is what he had done in
1915. Yet in that case—even though both the murder bullet and the test
bullet showed a characteristic imperfection—he was not willing to
state definitely that the murder bullet had been fired from the revolver
in evidence. He said instead that it was "consistent" with having been
fired from it. He used the same word in Dedham, stating that bullet III
was "consistent" with having been fired from Sacco's pistol. He admitted to the defense several years later that he had only meant, in using that word, that it had been fired from a pistol of the same type.

Evidence also indicates that Van Amburgh was initially unwilling to
go beyond such a statement. Posttrial statements by both Williams and
Proctor indicate that Van Amburgh was consulted because the prosecution was unhappy with Proctor's opinion as to bullet III and thought
that Van Amburgh might be able to give a more definite one.[20] Before
the trial, however, Van Amburgh, who had no previous experience in
criminal cases, was not willing to state that bullet III had definitely
come from Sacco's Colt. Thus Williams, in his opening statement and
in conversations with defense attorneys, made clear that the prosecution did not intend to claim that bullet III definitely matched Sacco's
pistol.

It is equally significant that the prosecution never requested permission to test-fire Sacco's Colt before the trial. They must not have done
so because they did not believe such a test could yield additional evidence. Bullet III—*whether genuine or not*—had a left twist, and Proctor
believed (mistakenly, as it developed at the trial) that only a Colt of all
.32 caliber automatics would give a bullet such a twist. On the other
hand, no test known to Proctor could match a bullet or shell to any particular .32 caliber automatic. No test, then, was necessary. If Van Am-

burgh had had a different view, he could have requested the test himself, yet it was an admitted fact that the prosecution had never made such a request. It was the defense that requested a test-firing, presumably because defense expert James Burns told Moore that he might be able to *rule out* the possibility that bullet III had come from Sacco's pistol. Before making this test the defense consulted with Sacco, who encouraged them to go ahead.[21] Even after the tests had been done Van Amburgh's trial testimony was only slightly more definite than Proctor's. Both men stated their opinion that the other five bullets had come from the same weapon, basing this conclusion on the similarity of the double set of rifling marks found upon them, and Proctor gave his opinion that that weapon had been a Savage automatic pistol. Proctor also stated that shell W appeared to come from the same make of weapon as test shells fired from Sacco's pistol and that bullet III was "consistent" with having been fired from that pistol. Van Amburgh was only slightly firmer; he said only that there was a "very strong similarity" between shell W and shells fired from Sacco's pistol and that he was "inclined to believe" that bullet III had come from Sacco's pistol.[22]

As a matter of fact, the reticence of both Proctor and Van Amburgh was fully justified by their knowledge—or rather their lack of knowledge—of the science of firearms. *The Identification of Firearms from Ammunition Fired Therein with an Analysis of Legal Authorities,* an early classic on the subject written by Jack Disbrow Gunther and Charles O. Gunther in 1935, includes a long analysis of the firearms evidence in the Sacco-Vanzetti case. The authors concluded, based on the testimony of Van Amburgh and Proctor, that neither one had any idea how to determine whether a bullet or shell had been fired from a particular pistol and that the markings Van Amburgh cited in an effort to tie the bullet and shell to Sacco's Colt were irrelevant to the issue at hand. Both had used inadequate equipment; neither had used a comparison microscope, the only tool enabling bullets to be identified with any certainty.[23] The defense testimony is shown to have been equally worthless.

"[Proctor's] redeeming quality," the Gunthers wrote, "was an apparent frankness."[24] It is clear from posttrial affidavits from Proctor, Katzmann, and Williams that Proctor told the prosecution he could not possibly testify that bullet III and shell W had definitely come from Sacco's gun, although he eventually agreed to use the word "consistent" in a misleading sense. Van Amburgh, whose knowledge was not significantly greater, must also have been initially unwilling to give a definite opinion, and even after the test-firing in June his trial testimony was only slightly more definite than Proctor's. Neither one was willing to state definitely that Sacco's pistol had fired them. (It is curious that Van Amburgh became much more definite after the trial and stated in a 1923 affidavit that he was "absolutely certain" that shell w had been fired from Sacco's pistol and "positive" that bullet III had been fired from it. These statements, however, were *also* based on an inadequate analysis evidence. It is possible that Van Amburgh simply believed that he had acquired enough technical knowledge to justify something that he had known all along. An affidavit submitted by another prosecution expert at that time, one Merton A. Robinson, merely restated Van Amburgh's reasoning.)[25]

Unfortunately for the defense, Williams, Katzmann, McAnarney, and Thayer managed to give the prosecution testimony far more significance than it warranted. To begin with, Williams phrased his questions to Proctor in such a way as to give the jury the impression that Proctor's use of the phrase "consistent with being fired from that pistol" meant that the bullet had indeed come from that pistol. Katzmann in his closing argument implied that Van Amburgh had given a firm opinion, and Thayer in his charge stated that *both* Van Amburgh and Proctor had testified to the effect that the bullet had been fired from Sacco's gun.[26] Katzmann also encouraged the jury to attempt to resolve the issue themselves by comparing shell w and bullet III to the test bullets and shells with a magnifying glass—a disgracefully prejudicial suggestion to have made, given that not even an expert could possibly make a proper determination in this way.

Thus, whoever perpetrated the switch did not do so in the belief that they had thereby created an unanswerable proof of Sacco's guilt. If indeed Proctor's initial examination of the bullets convinced him that all six of them—the four from Berardelli's body and the two from Parmenter's—had been fired from a Savage automatic, the prosecution probably reacted with intense frustration, since Stewart knew from his talk with Boda and his search of Puffer's Place that *Coacci*, whom the prosecution had always suspected of participating in the crime, had owned a Savage automatic. (To repeat, we now know that Proctor was wrong and that the bullets came from a Harrington and Richardson .32 caliber automatic.) The substitution of the bullet from Sacco's pistol simply made up for the failure to apprehend Coacci and his revolver. The substitution was not presumed to clinch the case and in this way was no more serious than much of the rest of the prosecution's tampering with the evidence. To claim falsely that Sacco's pistol *might* have fired one of the murder bullets was no more serious than to coax a reluctant identification witness, induce the arresting officers to testify that the defendants had tried to draw their guns, or claim in court that Frank Harding's slip of paper identifying the Bridgewater bandit car as a Hudson had been lost.

It remains to explain why Proctor, who in 1923 gave Defense Counsel William G. Thompson an affidavit indicating that his testimony at the trial had been wrongly interpreted, did not go further and admit the switch, which he must certainly have known about even if he was not responsible for it. Proctor's admission that by using the phrase "consistent with" having been fired from Sacco's pistol he did *not* mean to imply that he had found any evidence that it had come from that particular pistol made him something of a hero to Sacco and Vanzetti's defenders, and it opened up the prosecution to new charges of subornation of perjury. Yet it is clear that Proctor's affidavit has been misinterpreted, both by the defense and by some subsequent writers, and it is not at all surprising, given the circumstances of the affidavit and his overall role in the case, that he did not tell all he knew. Although Proctor had never believed Sacco and Vanzetti were guilty he had done little to prevent their conviction, and his main motive in undermining the prosecution seems to have been professional jealousy.

Proctor in 1923 first revealed his dissatisfaction with the prosecution to two defense experts, Albert Hamilton and Elias Field, who went to Proctor's house in Swampscott to examine the exhibits. Field subsequently drew up an affidavit describing the conversation, and the affidavit seems to have been based upon a three-page handwritten note deposited at Harvard Law School by the defense.[27] Proctor stated, according to the note, that he had never believed Sacco and Vanzetti were guilty and added somewhat disingenuously that he had been forced against his will to testify in the case. But the most obvious motive for his statements seems to have been resentment of Van Amburgh. "Mr. Van Amburgh," he is reported to have said, "testified to a lot of measurements he made. This was his first murder case & when he came here he did not know how to make those measurements until I showed him." Proctor added that, after he refused "most of a year" to give the opinion Katzmann wanted, "they got Mr. Van Amburgh who was willing & did give the desired opinion."

William G. Thompson approached Proctor later that year. He later told the Lowell Committee that Proctor was initially reluctant to swear an affidavit but finally decided to do so.[28] In his affidavit Proctor did *not* say, as some authors have implied, that he did not believe that bullet III had gone through Sacco's pistol or that his examinations had tended to persuade him that it had not. He stated merely that he had never found any evidence tending to persuade him that it had and that he had found Van Amburgh's arguments based upon the markings on the bullets "entirely unconvincing." Thus he had agreed with the district attorney (and he seems also to refer to Williams) upon the wording of his answer. In an answering affidavit Williams stated that it was Proctor who had suggested the use of the word "consistent," and since Proctor had previously used that word in another case there is every reason to believe that Williams was telling the truth. The affidavit and the handwritten note that predates it confirm that Proctor was angry at Van Amburgh mainly for having made a claim that he did not believe could be justified and perhaps for having supplanted Proctor as the leading Commonwealth firearms expert.[29]

Indeed, despite Proctor's often expressed belief in Sacco and Vanzetti's innocence, he had done little or nothing to prevent their conviction. Proctor never refused to continue the investigation of the South Braintree crime; it was Katzmann who dumped Proctor from the investigation after Vanzetti's Plymouth trial. At Plymouth Proctor gave knowingly misleading testimony, stating that the shell Dr. Murphy found on the street was "identical" to those found upon Vanzetti despite the difference in the weight of the shot. And although during the Dedham trial McAnarney heard Proctor remark in the corridor that the Commonwealth had not got the right men, Proctor never bothered to impart to the defense any of his devastating knowledge regarding the original testimony of the eyewitnesses or their identification of Palmisano's picture.[30] Nor did he suggest to McAnarney that the defense ask him what he meant by the use of the word "consistent," even though he later said that had the defense done so he would have replied that he had found no evidence to suggest that bullet III had gone through Sacco's pistol. Proctor, in short, played his hand very close to his chest.

Yet another account of Proctor's behavior at the time of the trial casts the gravest doubt upon his motives at that time. Testifying before the Lowell Committee in 1927, Katzmann claimed that Proctor had tried to collect a witness fee of five hundred dollars in compensation for his expert testimony at the trial and that Katzmann had refused to pay it.[31] The bulk of Katzmann's testimony before the committee is so obviously lacking in veracity that one cannot absolutely credit this story.

Among other things, he claimed not to remember what he knew about Sacco and Vanzetti's radical associations from conversations with federal agents; he denied knowing that several witnesses had identified pictures of Anthony Palmisano before Sacco's arrest; and he even denied remembering Henry Hellyer, the Pinkerton operative who wrote practically all the investigative reports on the South Braintree crime.[32] But if Katzmann's story regarding Proctor were true it would raise fascinating questions. Proctor's request for such a large sum of money (equal to several thousand 1982 dollars) in exchange for testimony not especially helpful to the prosecution could be interpreted as a request not simply to be paid but also to be paid off.

More than sixty years after the crime, it seems clear that the substitution of bullet III cannot *physically* be proven. In July 1982 Massachusetts Commissioner of Public Safety Frank J. Trabucco agreed to allow an examination of the four Berardelli bullets in an effort to determine if the three scratches on bullet III had indeed been made by a different instrument. The examination was conducted by Professor Regis Pelloux of the M.I.T. Metallurgy Department in his laboratory on 2 August 1982 in the presence of Lieutenant John McGuinness of the ballistics laboratory of the Department of Public Safety. Unfortunately, microscopic enlargements of the bullets were not conclusive. The appearance of the scratches on bullet III does differ somewhat from the other scratches, but the widths of the scratches vary widely from bullet to bullet. The difference in appearance could also be due, at least in part, to the deformation of bullet III, which may have made the metal somewhat harder and which left the surface of the base in a slightly concave state. The shape of the scratches suggests that they were made by similar sharp instruments, but beyond that nothing can be said. Photographs of the scratches are reproduced in figure 13.

Yet, despite the lack of conclusive physical proof, Dr. Magrath's grand jury testimony and Williams's handling of the bullets at the trial tend to confirm the eyewitness and autopsy evidence indicating that bullet III could not have been fired from a different gun and that a substitution must have taken place. From a strange source, moreover, comes evidence that such tampering with firearms evidence would hardly have been unique in contemporary Massachusetts. In 1946 the *Boston University Law Review* published "Common Sources of Error in the Examination and Interpretation of Ballistics Evidence" by none other than Charles Van Amburgh himself, who had died shortly before the publication of the article. The Sacco-Vanzetti case had made Van

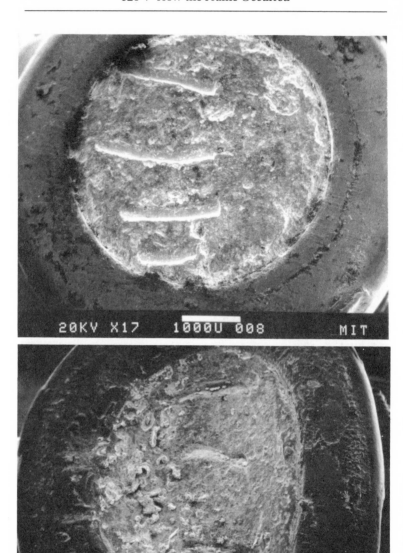

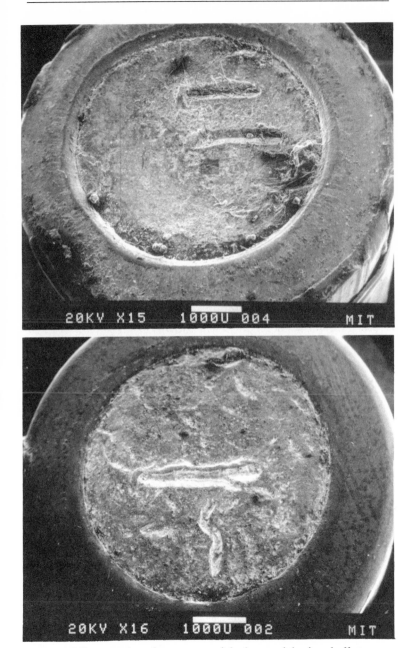

13. Microscopic enlargements of the bases of the four bullets introduced at the trial as having come from Berardelli's body. (Courtesy Professor Regis Pelloux, M.I.T.)

Amburgh's career. A few years later the Commonwealth had appointed him the first director of a new ballistics laboratory, a post he held for about two decades. Commenting on his long experience in 1946, Van Amburgh discussed problems in the proper handling and marking of exhibits.

> One old Medical Examiner refused to surrender a bullet for laboratory examination because thirty years before in the Eastman-Grogan case at Cambridge, Massachusetts, a bullet was stolen during a court proceeding in which he was a witness. It was necessary to persuade him through the District Attorney that times had changed and that he must surrender the exhibit. *It appears that the theft, substitution or defacement of exhibits was and is a sharp trick resorted to at times* [emphasis added].
>
> Many instances have appeared in the records where the failure to appoint an expert as custodian of exhibits has caused much delay in the trial of a defendant due to the defacing, larceny or misplacement of exhibits. Such incidents have been known to occur all too frequently. For example, in at least one murder case it was discovered that the barrel of the defendant's gun had been substituted.
>
> Episodes such as the above impelled the Massachustts authorities to take measures to protect exhibits from being defaced, lost, or stolen by appointing an expert on a full-time basis to handle ballistics exhibits and evidence connected therewith.
>
> It is a comparatively easy matter to betray the confidence of unsuspecting persons. It is too serious a matter to be left solely to persons who are unaware of the details and technical features of bullets, cartridge shells, and firearms.[33]

Well aware of the prevalence of shady practices, Van Amburgh seems never to have guessed that he began his own career as an unsuspecting person whose confidence was easily betrayed.

It is the great irony of the switch that its perpetrators did not understand the significance of the step they were taking. Had they understood that it would eventually be used to establish Sacco's guilt beyond any doubt, they might have shrunk from such a step. Instead, it was merely one of a long series of measures designed to insure that a jury would be persuaded to share their belief that they had caught the right men. It is a further irony that, had they substituted the Colt bullet for any bullet except III or I, it would not have been possible to have demonstrated the switch by virtue of the eyewitness and autopsy testimony. In this, however, historians are fortunate. The prosecution left a trail. It has thus been possible to establish, sixty years after the crime, that this, the most critical piece of evidence against the two men, was almost certainly as false as the rest.

11 / The Feds

n 1926 two former agents of the Bureau of Investigation, Frederick Weyand and Lawrence Leatherman, gave affidavits to William G. Thompson describing the role of the Bureau of Investigation (the ancestor of the FBI) in the Sacco-Vanzetti case. The affidavits seemed to confirm long-held beliefs among the Sacco-Vanzetti Defense Committee that the case had been a political frame-up from start to finish.

"Some time before the arrest of Sacco and Vanzetti on May 5, 1920," Weyand deposed, "—just how long before I do not remember—the names of both of them had got on the files of the Department of Justice as Radicals to be watched. . . . Both these men were listed in the files as followers or associates of an educated Italian editor named Galleani." Federal authorities, he continued, had not been involved in the arrest of Sacco and Vanzetti, but the Boston office had immediately begun closely watching the activities of the defense committee with the help of undercover agents, and Weyand and other agents had attended the Dedham murder trial for the purpose of gathering information about radical activities. A bureau spy, Carbone, had been placed in Dedham jail for the purpose of obtaining information from Sacco about either the Wall Street bombing of 16 September 1920 or the South Braintree murder but without result. "The understanding in this case between the agents of the Department of Justice in Boston and the District Attorney followed the usual custom," he continued, "that the Department of Justice would help the District Attorney to secure a conviction, and that he in turn would help the agents of the Department of Justice to secure information that they might desire." In particular, the department hoped to secure proof of Sacco and Vanzetti's anarchist beliefs as a basis for deporting them should they not be convicted of murder. Agent William West had exchanged information with Katzmann, including information on the defendants' radical activities to be used in their cross-examination. Weyand concluded that neither he nor any other agents of the Boston office involved in the case believed that Sacco and Vanzetti had had anything to do with the South Braintree crime, which in their opinion had been committed by "a gang of professional highwaymen."

Leatherman's affidavit noted that he had not joined the Boston office of the bureau until September 1921 but confirmed virtually everything that Weyand said. He added that correspondence and documents on file in the Boston office "would throw a great deal of light upon the preparation of the Sacco-Vanzetti case for trial, and upon the real opinion of the Boston office of the Department of Justice as to the guilt of Sacco and Vanzetti of the particular crime with which they were charged."[1]

Numerous appeals from Thompson and from Sacco-Vanzetti sympathizers around the country failed to persuade the Department of Justice to open its files on the case. Newly available FBI documents bearing on the case also show that William West, in a series of letters to FBI Director J. Edgar Hoover, denied most of Weyand and Leatherman's accusations and argued that the bureau had had nothing to do with the preparation of the case. Yet the files of the Bureau of Investigation—now available at the National Archives—clearly show, despite some tantalizing gaps, that a great deal of what Weyand and Leatherman said was true. As we have seen, the bureau had in its files the names of Sacco and Vanzetti in connection with a far-reaching investigation of the Galleani group of anarchists to which they belonged. Agents discussed the case with the Massachusetts State Police almost immediately after the 5 May arrest; a spy *was* placed in the Dedham jail to elicit information from Sacco; agents did attend the trial of Sacco and Vanzetti; and the activities of the defense committee were monitored with microscopic thoroughness. Available files contain only bits of information bearing directly upon the issue of the guilt or innocence of Sacco and Vanzetti, but they provide several fascinating pieces of information regarding the trial and leave some tantalizing questions regarding the federal government's role.

On 14 May 1920—nine days after the arrest of Sacco and Vanzetti—Boston Agent G. E. Kelleher received a visit from an unidentified "representative" of the Massachusetts State Police inquiring after Sacco and Vanzetti. A quick search of the files found Agent William West's report on the discovery of the *Cronaca Sovversiva* mailing list at the home of Augusto Rossi in Newton the preceding fall, and Kelleher located Sacco and Vanzetti's names on the list, thereby identifying them as Galleanisti. When the state officer mentioned that Vanzetti had gone to Mexico in 1917 Kelleher quickly uncovered West's reports on Carlo Valdinocci, the leader of the Mexico group of anarchists. Kelleher added that Agent W. E. Hill would continue to report on the case.[2]

At the time of Sacco and Vanzetti's arrest, the Boston office, as we have seen, was in the midst of a search for the perpetrators of the 2 June 1919 bombings. The arrest of two Galleanisti for robbery and murder might logically have spurred them to new efforts in this direction, but, curiously, Bureau of Investigation files show very little activity in this area in the late spring of 1920. An undated summary report of the Massachusetts federal agents' investigation into those bombings—apparently written in May or June of 1920—described the Bridgewater and South Braintree holdups, adding that "police authorities have recently arrested and held without bail one 'Bert' Vanzetti and one 'Mike' Sacco. This office has ascertained from its files that both of these men are of the Galleani group and further investigations are to be carried out along this line in the hope of securing some information in reference to the bomb plot."[3] No reports of further investigations, however, turn up for several months.

No available file contains any further Hill reports for some months, but 4 August and 10 August reports on radical activities in the Boston district described a series of meetings held on behalf of Sacco and Vanzetti. Agents had evidently been in touch with the two men's jailers; the report added that Vanzetti had received a letter from Carlo Tresca, the New York anarchist leader, requesting more money for Salsedo's defense fund.[4] Anarchists, who had been eclipsed by Communists on the Boston office's horizon after 1918, were becoming the focus of renewed interest.

On 16 September 1920 a horse-drawn wagon exploded at noon at the corner of Broad and Wall streets, New York, directly opposite the offices of J. P. Morgan and Company. Thirty-three people were killed and several hundred injured by pieces of shrapnel, and police quickly concluded that the wagon, whose driver had apparently abandoned it several minutes earlier, had carried a large bomb. William J. Flynn, director of the Bureau of Investigation, descended upon New York at once and on 17 September announced the finding of five circulars in a mailbox near the explosion, which read "Remember We will not tolerate any longer. Free the political prisoners or it will be sure death for all of you. American Anarchist Fighters." Both the printing and the signature, Flynn said, resembled the "Plain Words" handbill found at the sites of the 2 June 1919 bombings. In an interview with a Chicago correspondent, Flynn specifically blamed the Galleani gang for the bombing, stating (incorrectly) that Carlo Tresca had replaced Galleani as the leader of the group.[5] New York agents activated all their contacts among local anarchists.[6] The bureau began the tedious process of checking out stores at which sets of rubber stamps that might have been used to print the leaflets had been sold.

Although in public Flynn quickly backed away from these accusations, he seems to have decided that the bomb had been set in retaliation for the arrest of Sacco and Vanzetti. The Boston office was immediately put to work on this hypothesis, and on 24 September Agent West reported that his investigations had led him to believe that Aldino Felicani, the treasurer of the Sacco-Vanzetti Defense Committee, was now the leader of New England anarchists.[7] On 11 October the New York office asked for information on Sacco and Vanzetti, adding that according to West—then on assignment in New York—Agent William Hill had been making reports on the Sacco-Vanzetti case. Hill replied that Sacco had been arrested in Milford in 1916 and convicted of disturbing the peace, for which he had paid a fine.[8] On 15 October another Boston agent found a stamp dealer who recalled having sold a set of the telltale rubber stamps to two foreigners in late July or early August. His description of one of them seemed to match that of Felicani, but when given an opportunity covertly to view Felicani the salesman said that he had not been the purchaser.[9]

In November 1920 Agent West, in a further attempt to develop information on the Wall Street bombing, arranged with Katzmann and with Sheriff Capen of Dedham to place an undercover agent, Carbone, in a jail cell next to Sacco. On 30 November Carbone reported that Sacco had told him, in a conversation in the jail yard, "that he was an anarchist, that he was against the capitalist, but that he had never killed any man, and that he would be proven innocent of the crime with which he is charged when his case comes to trial next month." Sacco added that a Braintree shoe repairman knew who had actually done the shooting. In a note Sacco had repeated that he was innocent, adding, "They have accused me of having committed a terrible crime, simply because I have been the defender of the workers and also because I am an Italian." By 1 December Sacco had become suspicious of Carbone, and Carbone was removed a few days later.[10] On 13 January 1921 Moore wrote the Boston office, making it clear that he knew about Carbone and requesting an explanation. Charles Hanrahan, the agent in charge of the Boston office, refused to reply in writing.[11] Continuing to monitor developments in the case, Agent Hill subsequently attended the De Falco trial in January 1921.[12]

Neither the New York nor the Boston office seems to have turned up anything further linking any Galleanisti to the Wall Street bombing, but the Boston office used the agitation surrounding Sacco and Vanzetti to gather new information on local radicals. Aldino Felicani became their principal target. Beginning in early November 1920, Boston agents secured search warrants allowing them to open and read his mail, and undercover agents observed the committee's activities as closely as possible.[13] Every letter Felicani received from November through the time of the trial was opened, read, and sent to Washington. The letters detailed the committee's attempts to raise money in anarchist and labor circles all over the country on behalf of the two men. Money rolled in at the rate of several hundred dollars a week.[14] The mail cover provided the basis for further investigations. In June 1921 agents read a letter to Felicano from Joseph Russo, an anarchist who had taken over the printing press of the *Cronaca Sovversiva* in Providence, Rhode Island, and shipped it to Italy. In a letter from Nevada, Russo protested that he had been a loyal anarchist for many years and that he had the correspondence to prove it. San Francisco agents promptly arrested Russo and seized his records.[15] In August of 1921 Bureau of Investigation Chief Flynn, shortly to be removed, stated his intention of investigating *every* contributor to the Sacco-Vanzetti defense fund.[16]

Still hopeful of turning up information on the Wall Street bombing or of identifying prominent radicals, the New York office of the bureau in June 1921 dispatched an undercover agent, Joseph Barbera, to attend the trial. His reports give a fascinating picture of the courtroom atmosphere. On 2 June, during the extremely lengthy process of picking the jury, he speculated that jurors were afraid to sit on the case for fear of reprisal. Dedham Chief of Police Shine told him that "Sacco and Vanzetti are two of the worst radicals in Massachusetts and would be liable to commit any crime"; Shine added that Orciani must have driven the South Braintree bandit car and that he still hoped to connect him to the crime. Bureau Agent Hanrahan feared that the defense would call the spy Carbone to the stand. On 8 June Barbera wrote that Dedham was "filled with state officers from Boston and all cities and towns near Dedham"; he himself had run-ins with police officers several times daily, and while he had not yet disclosed his identity he might soon be forced to, "to safeguard myself. The feeling in Dedham against Italians is very strong, and will probably get stronger as the trial progresses."

On 13 June Barbera submitted his most interesting report. "It is agent's opinion," he wrote, "there will be no radical demonstration as the prosecution has presented a poor case against the subjects, and all of the witnesses thus far called, with the exception of one, have identified Sacco as being at the scene of the crime, but the testimony was badly shaken by the cross examination of counsel for the defense." (Actually, as of 12 June, only Wade, Splaine, Pelser, and Andrews, among the identification witnesses, had taken the stand.) Judge Thayer's bodyguard had told him that Thayer himself had remarked during lunch "that the prosecution has a weak case and he did not think that Sacco and Vanzetti would be convicted on the evidence thus far presented." Felicani also believed that the men were receiving a fair trial and that they would be acquitted.[17] Unfortunately, Barbera was asked to return home one or two days later.

Boston agents continued to keep Washington informed of the trial, but available reports do not indicate their opinion of the evidence. On 8 July Agent Hanrahan wrote J. Edgar Hoover and listed the names of the anarchists who had testified on behalf of the defense. Another Boston agent, Di Lillo, continued to attend the trial on orders of William West, and on 27 July he described the testimony of Sacco and Vanzetti, including the anarchist friends they had identified.[18] The bureau continued to follow the activities of the defense committee even more closely after the conviction of the two men. Washington feared an eruption of violence should they be executed, and on 9 November 1921 the new director of the bureau, William J. Burns, asked for *daily* reports on the agitation. These reports continued until March 1922; some were submitted by Lawrence Leatherman, who subsequently gave William Thompson an affidavit describing the bureau's interest in the case. During this period the Boston office remained in close touch with the district attorney's office for the purpose of following the progress of appeals in the case.[19]

The bureau intermittently monitored the progress of the case and the agitation surrounding the appeals until July 1926, when Thompson, who had in the meantime secured Weyand and Leatherman's affidavits, wrote the attorney general of the United States asking for access to the files of the Boston office. Hoover—now the director of the Bureau of Investigation—forwarded this request to John A. Dowd, now director of the Boston office. Dowd consulted with Harold Williams—now the U.S. attorney in Boston—and Williams argued against releasing any material from the files. Dowd fully understood that Thompson wanted to explain the defendants' behavior on the night of their arrest on grounds that they feared arrest by federal authorities; as he informed Hoover, however, Agent West denied having heard of either defendant before their arrest. West claimed, in fact, that the Boston office had not even known of the arrests of Elia and Salsedo in New York, but since Agent M. J. Davis had gone to Boston in March 1920 immediately after their arrest this seems impossible. West did not deny that the names of Sacco and Vanzetti might have appeared in some earlier reports in Boston office files—as indeed they had—but Dowd added that "they were certainly not sufficiently active to come to the attention of the office up to that time in any matter of importance."[20]

The critical accusation in Weyand and Leatherman's affidavits was of course that federal agents had assisted in the preparation of the prosecution's case, and Dowd handled it with extreme care. Confirming that a "comity of interests" frequently existed between state and local authorities, he added that this case had been "within the jurisdiction of the state solely" and that "even if assistance was asked, this office would not be in a position, if allowed, to furnish a man or men experienced in the investigation of murder cases." Not until November or December of 1920 had *Mr. West* "conferred with District Attorney Katzmann," and then only in relation to the Carbone matter. (West himself was the source of this information.)[21] While perhaps true, these statements do not, as we shall see, dispose of the matter. A subsequent letter denied that West had ever attended the trial, as reported by Weyand, or that Katzmann had ever asked for information about the defendants' radical activities to use in cross-examination.[22] On 1 October 1926 Dowd forwarded a complete summary of the Boston office files relating to the case to Hoover.

As the execution date for Sacco and Vanzetti approached in the summer of 1927, the Department of Justice and the bureau were deluged with requests to open the files, but Hoover consistently refused to do so and satisfied the acting attorney general, G. R. Farnum, that nothing in the files related to Sacco and Vanzetti.[23] Hoover seems above all to have been anxious to avoid the impression of any impropriety on the part of the bureau, an attitude he steadfastly maintained during the whole of his forty-seven-year tenure as director.

Based on these statements and on other material from the files, then, it appears that Weyand and Leatherman's affidavits, while true in some respects, were false on several critical points. Weyand was correct that the names of Sacco and Vanzetti had come to the Boston office's attention on several occasions before their arrest. The department was *not* actively seeking them at the time of their arrest, but as we saw earlier, its bombing investigations were crossing the two men's paths.[24] Weyand's information regarding the informant in the Dedham jail was accurate. The key points at issue were the question of cooperation between the Boston office and the district attorney's office and the agents' opinion as to the guilt of Sacco and Vanzetti.

It seems, in fact, that Dowd and West did not tell the whole truth about the Boston office's involvement in the case. Several times in their correspondence with Hoover they stated that the first document in their files relating to the case dated from the fall of 1920, when the New York office asked for information on Sacco and Vanzetti. This was not true. We have seen that the case was called to the attention of the Boston office less than ten days after the arrests, on 14 May 1920, when Agent Kelleher received a visit from an unidentified state police officer. Kelleher's report was still on file in Washington in 1927 (and remains in the National Archives today), but it did *not* appear in a complete summary of the Boston files relating to the Sacco-Vanzetti case prepared by the Boston office in 1927. Kelleher noted that Agent William Hill would continue to follow the case, and five months later, on 11 October, the New York office asked for information on Sacco and Vanzetti, adding that according to West—then on assignment in New York—Hill *had been making reports on the Sacco-Vanzetti case.*[25] But no reports from Hill from this period survive.[26] Several files listed in the subsequent summary of Boston office files bear the notation, "Nothing in file; contents removed."[27] The Boston office's interrogation of Felicani in March of 1920 has not survived.

In retrospect, it would seem somewhat extraordinary if the Boston office had *not* taken a greater interest in the case. The office immediately determined that Sacco and Vanzetti were Galleanisti—that is, members of a group long sought by the bureau and at that very moment the target of a new investigation concerning the bombings of 2 June 1919. A thorough search through the files of the Boston office would also have shown that the two men were fairly prominent within the group, having been among those who traveled to Mexico with Valdinocci in 1917. The possibility that members of the group had executed a fifteen-thousand-dollar robbery would presumably have been of considerable interest. And indeed, some bureau reports suggest that their backgrounds *were* thoroughly looked into. A summary of the case submitted in October 1921 recounted their prearrest lives in considerable detail and included several facts that had not emerged in the trial. Vanzetti in particular was identified as a contributor to and distributor of the *Cronaca Sovversiva* who had received one hundred copies a week.[28]

During the trial, Katzmann received some information regarding Sacco's radical activities from Alfred Becker, the New York attorney who had apparently assisted Massachusetts authorities in their investigation of the 1919 bombings. Becker passed on and embellished information from the informer Ravarini, who in December 1919 had visited New England and spoken with Saverio Piesco, a leading Milford anarchist and a friend of Sacco's. According to Ravarini, Piesco recalled that Sacco had berated him (Piesco) after Piesco had attempted to show that an explosion in Franklin, Massachusetts, sometime earlier had been set off by the police rather than by anarchists.[29] While cross-examining Sacco, Katzmann asked if he knew Piesco, and when Sacco said he did, Katzmann said, "Do you remember two or three years ago the fact that there was a bomb explosion at Franklin about some holiday, and I think either Thanksgiving or Christmas Day?" McAnarney objected, and after an unreported conference at the bench Katzmann dropped this line of questioning. Katzmann apparently received other information on radical activity as well. When Sacco admitting subscribing to the *Cronaca Sovversiva*, Katzmann identified it as having been suppressed during the war.[30] Testifying before the Lowell Committee in 1927, Katzmann did indicate that he knew something about Galleani.[31]

The prosecution may have used Sacco and Vanzetti's association with Galleani, whose adherents law enforcement officers had publicly accused of the Wall Street and June 1919 bombings, to extort from the defense the remarkable stipulation that Katzmann read to the jury on 1 July 1921, the twenty-seventh day of the trial.

> The Commonwealth assents to the request of both of the defendants that all evidence heretofore offered in the course of this trial to the effect that either or both of said defendants bore the reputation of being peaceful and law-abiding citizens be stricken from the record of this trial, and that such evidence heretofore offered be entirely disregarded by the jury, so that as a result of striking the same from the record there is no evidence before the jury that either or both of said defendants bore the reputation of being a peaceful and law-abiding citizen.[32]

Traditionally, this stipulation has been explained as follows: at the beginning of the trial Katzmann had agreed to exclude evidence of Vanzetti's conviction at Plymouth in exchange for the defense's withholding evidence of good character with respect to Vanzetti, if not Sacco, and that Katzmann had secured this new stipulation during the trial after

McAnarney had called a Plymouth policeman who attested to Vanzetti's good reputation. Even with respect to Vanzetti this was a bad bargain, since the jurors could easily have known about his previous conviction anyway. But why was it necessary to include Sacco as well? It is curious that, in testimony before the Lowell Committee in 1927, neither Thomas McAnarney, who assisted his brother during the trial, nor Katzmann remembered that the stipulation applied to both defendants.[33] We cannot know, at this time, whether the prosecution used the threat of tying them to sensational bombing incidents to strike out their character witnesses.

Weyand and Leatherman had been dismissed from the bureau in 1924.[34] Undoubtedly they wrote with some bitterness, and their statements were inaccurate in several particulars. Still, there was plenty of truth to what they said, and surviving files may not tell the whole story. It seems, first of all, that Agent Hill did follow the case more closely than surviving records indicate, although he may have limited his contacts to the investigating officers rather than the district attorney's office itself. Second, the Boston office might well have lost interest in the matter in the summer of 1920 because they had indeed concluded that Sacco and Vanzetti were not guilty of murder and that the crime, as Weyand and Leatherman said, had probably been committed by professional highwaymen. Very little in the files bears directly upon the guilt of Sacco and Vanzetti, but the files confirm the federal government's interest in anarchist activities of all kinds. Unfortunately, any more significant information that may have been in the files seems to be lost forever.

12 / Alternative Theories

The prósecution and those authors who have supported part or all of its case have always contended that Sacco and Vanzetti were part of a larger conspiracy whose members they had identified, even though the other bandits escaped arrest and conviction. The defense, on the other hand, believed by 1926 that it had identified the real perpetrators of the crime, the Morelli gang of Providence, Rhode Island, and research into the Morelli hypothesis continued long after Sacco and Vanzetti's execution. Here again new evidence allows for a reevaluation of both of these theories.

In his opening statement Assistant District Attorney Harold Williams implicated Coacci and Boda definitely and Orciani more vaguely in the crime. The jury was shown the house at Puffer's Place where Boda and Coacci had lived, and Katzmann in his closing argument stressed that the abandoned Buick had been found less than two miles away from it. In a sense this was logical. Stewart in late April and early May of 1920 had begun suspecting the anarchists after Coacci's precipitous departure on 16 April, and he had really been after Boda on the night of 5 May. But it seems almost impossible, for various reasons, that Orciani or Coacci took part in the South Braintree murder and robbery. Boda is a slightly more suspicious figure.

We have seen, to begin with, that while Orciani was apprehended and actually identified by witnesses as having been present at South Braintree he was released in May 1920 because the pay sheets at the Norwood foundry where he worked showed that he had been there on that day.[1] The prosecution never believed this evidence, and Katzmann made clear to the Lowell Committee in 1927 that he did not believe that Orciani himself had punched the clock.[2] It must, however, be assumed that the prosecution went to the factory to find whether Orciani might have put such a subterfuge across on 15 April and found no evidence that he did. Several decades later a journalist, Thomas O'Connor, recalled that the Plympton Foundry where Orciani worked employed only twenty or twenty-five men and that they had fiercely resisted efforts by the prosecution to break down his alibi.[3] According to Robert D'Attilio, Orciani was an active anarchist of long standing who had known Sacco in Milford and whose name had appeared in the *Cronaca Sovversiva*.[4]

Mike Boda was of all known associates of Sacco and Vanzetti the most suspicious. While Coacci, Sacco, and Orciani had factory jobs and Vanzetti peddled fish, Boda described himself to Michael Stewart as a salesman of Italian foods but later confessed to being a bootlegger. He too, however, seems to have been an active anarchist who was arrested in a 1916 antiwar demonstration and went to Mexico in 1917 to avoid the draft.[5] Mussolini's Fascist government also seems to have identified him as an active anarchist and imprisoned him in the late 1920s. Previously, after living in various parts of the United States, running a laundry in Wellesley, Massachusetts, and making the trip to Mexico, Boda in the fall of 1919 had begun living with the Coaccis at Puffer's Place.

Boda initially attracted Stewart's attention because he was an anarchist who owned an automobile and lived less than two miles from the spot that the Buick used in the South Braintree murders was found. Indeed, Katzmann and Stewart firmly believed that the Buick found in the Manley Woods had been stolen by Boda and used in both the Bridgewater and the South Braintree holdup attempts. The prosecution further claimed that Boda had kept the Buick in the same shed behind his house in which he had kept his Overland. In fact, available evidence tends to show quite definitely that no Buick ever was kept in that shed. Three neighbors, including one woman who had ridden in Boda's car, told the defense that they had never seen any car but the Overland that went to Simon Johnson's shop either in Puffer's Place or with Boda at the wheel.[6] In 1927 Samuel Johnson, brother of Simon Johnson, said that as a postman he had sometimes looked inside Boda's garage during the late winter of 1920 and that he had never seen anything but an Overland.[7] Two other neighbors, on the other hand, did say that they had seen Boda *driving* a Buick. One was the fourteen-year-old Napoleon Enscher, whose testimony at the Bridgewater trial was most unconvincing. The other neighbor was Paul MacDonald, a seventeen-year-old boy who delivered milk to Boda and the Coaccis. Interviewed by Defense Attorney Callahan on 28 December 1920, MacDonald remembered his Italian customers warmly. He confirmed that he had never seen any car but the Overland at Puffer's Place but maintained very definitely that on two occasions, which he could not date precisely, he had also seen Boda driving a Buick.[8] In 1928, while imprisoned on the island of Lipari, Boda spoke at length to Edward Houlton James, a case aficionado who had carefully read the defense papers relating to him. Boda bluntly denied Enscher's and MacDonald's statements, saying that he had never driven any car but his own Overland.[9]

In *Tragedy in Dedham* Francis Russell implied that Boda's Spanish automatic might have fired the five right-twist bullets recovered from Parmenter's and Berardelli's bodies.[10] This theory was consistent with the firearms evidence as understood at the time, but we have seen that more recent investigations have concluded that a .32 Harrington and Richardson automatic fired those bullets. Boda's distinctive appearance also makes him a somewhat unlikely participant in the crime. He was only five feet, two or three inches, tall and weighed about 120 pounds, with a mustache, and virtually all the witnesses to the crime described men of medium size and build. The prosecution had to admit to Judge Thayer that they had no witnesses who could place anyone of Boda's description in South Braintree on the day of the crime. Thayer for this reason excluded the Enscher testimony placing Boda at the wheel of a Buick car.[11] He clearly was *not* the thin, blond man who drove the bandit car in South Braintree.

On the surface Coacci, who sailed for Italy in April 1920, seems a more likely criminal. He had worked at Slater and Morrill; his trunk, opened by police after his departure, contained some shoe parts that he had apparently stolen; and his description—dark, stocky, and clean-shaven—would fit numerous descriptions of the bandits.[12] But although Coacci's tenure at Slater and Morrill raises the possibility that he helped plan the robbery, it effectively rules him out as a participant. Coacci had quit Slater and Morrill in early April 1920 after working there for almost three years. It is almost impossible that he could have hung around South Braintree and lounged by the fence on Pearl Street before the shooting without being recognized and most unlikely that Parmenter, who said before he died that he did not know his assailants, would not have known who he was.[13]

An extraordinary statement in the defense files also casts considerable doubt on any involvement by Boda or Coacci. On 24 December 1920, Moore interviewed Joseph Ventola, a courthouse worker, interpreter, and bail bondsman. Many months before the crime, Ventola explained, Coacci's brother-in-law had asked him to post Coacci's thousand-dollar bond to avoid immediate deportation, and Ventola, who did not know Coacci at all, agreed. On 15 April—the day Coacci was to present himself for deportation—the immigration authorities reached Ventola and explained that Coacci, not having appeared, was likely to forfeit his bond. Ventola immediately went to Bridgewater to find out what had happened, arriving at Puffer's Place at about four o'clock. Only Mrs. Coacci was home, and she explained that Coacci was looking for a woman to take care of her after he left. (The story Coacci told the immigration inspector on 16 April, that he had not presented himself because of his wife's illness, seems to have been true; Ventola and several other acquaintances confirmed that she was often sick.) Between four and five in the afternoon Ventola saw Boda walking toward the house from town—the opposite direction from the Manley Woods, where the bandit car was found two days later. Boda was carrying a black bag that appeared to be almost empty, seemed perfectly calm, and had no private conversation with Mrs. Coacci.[14]

We have seen that Sacco, Vanzetti, Boda, Coacci, and Orciani were dedicated, active anarchists, and had they committed a robbery they would almost surely have done so for political reasons. What little we know of their activities in the months before the crime does not, however, suggest any motivation for such a crime. Of particular interest are four letters and a card that Vanzetti wrote to Aldino Felicani in Boston between December 1919 and April 1920. The first *does* involve large sums of money; it includes a circular describing the plans of Italian comrades attempting to start an anarchist daily and their attempt to collect from American comrades between three thousand and forty-five hundred dollars with which to purchase a linotype machine. One might naturally wonder whether a few zealous comrades might have decided to resort to direct action to collect the money from the capitalist class, but thanks to the mail cover maintained by federal agents upon the Sacco-Vanzetti Defense Committee, we know that this was not the case. The February 1921 issue of *Spartaco*, an Italian anarchist monthly, included a letter from a Boston anarchist, F. Colarossi, whose name came up at the trial of Sacco and Vanzetti. He too referred to the subscription designed to raise money for the linotype and specified that it was destined for *Umanità Nuova*, a Milan daily published by the leading Italian anarchist, Errico Malatesta. Colarossi explained that to date American comrades had collected seven hundred dollars but that they had now decided to turn the money over to the Sacco-Vanzetti Defense Committee.[15] Indeed, Italian-American anarchists frequently collected money by subscription to support strikes or comrades in trouble—most notably during the Sacco-Vanzetti case itself.

Vanzetti's second letter, written on 26 March 1921, apparently deals with dissent within the anarchist community. Written in a highly cryptic style, it discusses the activities of an unnamed comrade, "T," and the need to discuss him with "Ligio"—perhaps Galleani himself, now in Italy. The third, on 12 April—just three days before the South Braintree murders—enclosed an article written by Vanzetti, one dealing in part with "the agrarian problem," almost certainly a reference to Italian conditions. The article may well have been destined for an Italian publication. The fourth, on 17 April, reports word from Salsedo received through another comrade, one Luigi Falzini, and describes Salsedo's need for money. The last, a card written on 23 April, looks forward to a meeting at Boni's restaurant, the anarchist hangout in the North End, on Sunday, 27 April.[16]

Although Vanzetti, at approximately the time of the crime, was looking for money to help Salsedo and Elia, it seems quite clear that money from the Slater and Morrill payroll did *not* go for this purpose. As we have seen, Vanzetti did travel to New York between the time of the crime and the time of his arrest, but when the prosecution followed up this trail it discovered a dead end. On 22 August 1927, the day of the execution, the *Boston Traveler* printed a story based on a briefing from a Justice Department official. It stated that after Sacco and Vanzetti's arrest the prosecution had asked the Boston office of the Department of Justice if radical groups had recently come into large sums of money. The Boston office queried the New York office to ask whether the Italian Workers' Defense League, which had concerned itself with the fate of Salsedo and Elia, had received any large sums of money in late April or early May 1920. The New York office had an informant among the leaders of this league, a man who spoke almost daily with its principal figure, Carlo Tresca, but the answer was that no such sum had been received. At the trial the defense also introduced a fifty-dollar money order that Vanzetti had sent to the Salsedo defense committee in New York on 30 April, immediately after he had returned from New York to Boston. It seems unlikely that he would have done this had he just delivered fifteen thousand dollars in cash.[17] There is, in short, no even remotely complete theory to explain exactly how and why anarchists including Sacco and Vanzetti might have committed the South Braintree robbery and murder.

Other theories involving other criminals, however, proliferated from the beginning. The defense papers now available at the Boston Public Library show that Fred Moore put a high priority, both before and after the trial, upon following up any tip that might lead the defense to other perpetrators of either the Bridgewater or the South Braintree holdup. One promising suspect, who surfaced in 1922, was William Dodson, a professional car thief arrested and jailed in 1921 for stealing Judge Thayer's car. In November 1921, federal agents learned that Dodson's wife, then in the midst of a divorce action, claimed that he had told her that he had driven the South Braintree bandit car. Agents promptly investigated Dodson, who promptly denied it, and eventually concluded that his wife, Josie May Henry, was so unreliable that no credence could be placed in her statement. They also discovered that Dodson was a mulatto, who clearly did not match the description of the blond driver of the bandit car.[18]

In the spring of 1922 defense investigators picked up the story and talked twice with Josie May Henry, Dodson's former wife. She told them that Dodson had confessed to her that he had taken part in the South Braintree robbery and that the police were wrong about Sacco and Vanzetti, but she could not date this remark with any precision. She added that her husband was a car thief who stored stolen cars around Needham and Newton, a promising lead indeed, since it was from this area that both the Buick and the license plates used in the South Braintree holdup had been taken. Moore eventually found the garage where Dodson had stashed his cars in April 1920, but its proprietor, a Mrs. Scully, remembered his having only Fords there. When a defense investigator interviewed Dodson in Charlestown State Prison, he made a striking discovery: "Physically he was almost the exact duplicate of Sacco in height, weight, general build, complexion, color of hair and color of eyes." Dodson seemed concerned about his wife's statements; he denied them, adding that the only Buick he had ever stolen was the one that belonged to Judge Thayer.[19] His description seems to rule out Dodson as the *driver* of the bandit car in South Braintree, but he could have participated in the crime. Curiously, he drove Judge Thayer's car, which he stole in Worcester, to Providence—the same direction taken by the South Braintree bandit car.[20]

Several eyewitnesses to the South Braintree robbery and murder had speculated that Berardelli had known the bandits. Only this, they felt, would have explained the robbers' determination to kill him. The defense did not pursue this theory at the trial, but in the posttrial period investigators did turn up some highly suggestive information about the murdered guard. After making his living as a barber in Connecticut and Massachusetts for some years, Berardelli had in 1919 been hired by the Watts Detective Agency in Boston. W. J. Watts, a former chief police inspector in Boston, discussed his employment with a defense investigator on 4 November 1921.

Stated that Alexandra [sic] Berardelli was employed by him from March 6th to March 26th, inclusive, 1919. That he dis-

charged Berardelli for dishonesty and unsatisfactory character. He
said that Berardelli worked as an operative for him on a case
which involved the handling of some money. That Berardelli did
not make a truthful report on the same. Also that he did not return
money which he should have and that when he left he failed to
square up account with the agency.[21]

Shortly afterward, Berardelli went to work with another private investigator, Frederick Webster, whom defense investigator Robert Reid
interviewed on 29 March 1921. Webster claimed to have placed Berardelli in "Rice & Hutchins," where he investigated shoe thefts; it seems
from other sources that he must have meant Slater and Morrill. Webster
was apparently no stickler for professional ethics. In the fall of 1919, at
about the time that Slater and Morrill hired Berardelli, he was hired by
the Boston police force after the mass firings that ended the Boston police strike. Within a year he had been arrested, convicted, and jailed for
participating in robberies.[22]

Defense investigators heard even more suggestive stories from two
former neighbors of the Berardellis in Quincy. Mrs. Aldeah Florence,
who had testified briefly at the trial regarding Berardelli's revolver, told
a much longer story to Fred Moore on 1 December 1921. She claimed
to have been easily the Berardellis' closest friend while they lived in
Quincy and continued as follows:

She says that on the night of April 14th they were all together and
were indulging in some jocularity and play. That Mr. Berardelli
said that they were having too good a time, that something was
likely to happen or something to that general effect. He said that
he felt too happy to have it continue.

On the morning of April 15th Mr. Berardelli left the house at
6:30, going away before his usual hour, which was 7 o'clock. She
said, however, that later her husband met Berardelli over at the
station.

She stated that during the morning Mrs. Berardelli came over to
the house and that she appeared to be depressed and said that she
was worried. She said that Mr. Berardelli had kissed her that
morning before he went away, the first time in many months.
Also that he had said that when their little daughter, Ida, who was
at that time in the hospital, came home that Mrs. Berardelli was
to give her the very best care and attention and further stated as

he went away that he hoped that everything would come out all right. Mrs. Berardelli said to Mrs. Florence that she could not understand what it all meant. Mrs. Florence stated that Mrs. Berardelli was apparently very much worried over his attitude and said that she was sure something was going to happen that day.[23]

While on the face of it this story seems more than a mite too pat, it had, unbeknownst to the defense, already received the most powerful corroboration. When Michael Stewart first interviewed Mrs. Berardelli in January 1921 she told him her husband had been worrying about bad men around the factory for about one week before he was killed. On the day of the robbery he had left the house at 5:30, two hours earlier than he had ever left before, and said he had something to do. "I am no coward," she reported him to have said, "and I am going to stay on the job." She thought that "black hand men" had committed the crime.[24] Perhaps he merely suspected trouble; perhaps he knew more.

The various defense investigations failed, however, to come up with a comprehensive theory until late 1925, when Celestino Madeiros actually confessed to participating in the crime. Madeiros, a Portuguese-American criminal in his early twenties, found himself in Dedham jail, where Sacco was still incarcerated, in 1925. In November of the previous year he had shot and killed a bank cashier during a holdup in nearby Wrentham. Represented by Francis Squires, he had been convicted of first-degree murder in 1925. His case was being appealed in late 1925 when he passed a note to Sacco confessing his participation in the South Braintree murder. In a subsequent affidavit taken by William G. Thompson, Madeiros said he had been in the bandit car together with a gang of Italians from Providence and described their movements on the day of the robbery. (Later he indicated that the driver was pale, blond, and not Italian—facts confirming numerous eyewitness descriptions.) Although Madeiros, whose mind worked according to his own peculiar but consistent logic, refused to name any confederates, he mentioned that they had made their living robbing freight cars near Providence. Thompson detailed another attorney, Herbert Ehrmann, to investigate his story. Ehrmann's investigations, which he described in great detail in his book *The Untried Case*, uncovered a series of amazing coincidences.

The Morelli gang of Providence fits Madeiros's description in every particular—and then some. Not only had they robbed freight cars, but on 15 April 1920 most of them had been out on bail awaiting trial for such robberies. The indictments charged them with stealing shoe shipments from Rice and Hutchins, another South Braintree factory adjacent to Slater and Morrill, indicating their familiarity with South Braintree and suggesting, as gang leader Joe Morelli later confirmed, that a spotter must have informed them when shipments went out. The same spotter could easily have alerted them to the possibility of taking the payroll.

Madeiros himself steadfastly refused to name the Morellis as his confederates, but he admitted knowing them when Thompson took his deposition in June 1926. And James Weeks, Madeiros's confederate in the Wrentham holdup, swore that Madeiros had described both his own and the Morellis' involvement in the South Braintree crime in several conversations. Another old acquaintance of Madeiros, one Barney Monterio, confirmed this as well.[25]

After long talks with Providence law enforcement officers, Ehrmann eventually concluded that the murder party had included three of the Morelli brothers, Madeiros, a blond driver named Steve Benkovsky who had subsequently been killed, and Anthony Mancini, well known to be the most dangerous member of the Morelli gang. Ehrmann thought that Joe Morelli, the eldest brother, had planned the robbery; Mancini, who had owned a .32 European automatic that defense experts believed might have fired the five right-twist bullets taken from the two guards, he tabbed as the trigger man. The Morellis seem to have been a prominent organized-crime family. In February 1921 Mancini, who had managed to avoid arrest in connection with the freight-car robberies, killed one Anthony Alterio in front of a New York police station. Contemporary press reports named Alterio as the leader of the American branch of Camorra, a Neapolitan crime brotherhood; certainly a substantial figure, Alterio left an estate of almost $150,000. New York police said Mancini had shot him at the behest of a Providence gang—quite possibly the Morellis—whom Alterio had refused to help in some unspecified matter.[26] Joe Morelli turned out to bear a striking resemblance to Sacco, and several of the witnesses who had failed to identify Sacco or Vanzetti identified his picture as one of the bandits.[27] Others said that photos of Benkovsky and Mancini resembled men they had seen. Years later Ben Bagdikian, a reporter for the *Providence Journal*, discovered that the Providence police had also suspected the Morellis of the South Braintree crime at the time it took place.

Despite provocative prison interviews with Joe Morelli and Mancini, Ehrmann never secured any further confessions or physical proof of their involvement. Madeiros's story, however, was corroborated by a great deal of evidence that he could not possibly have known about.

Madeiros said that he had been picked up in Providence at 4:00 A.M. by the gang in a Hudson car and that they had met another gang member in the woods near Randolph, Massachusetts, and changed there to a Buick brought by that man. The unidentified man remained behind to look after the Hudson. They had driven immediately to a saloon in South Boston where the gang received some information about the payroll. He said they had returned then to Providence (later he suggested they had not gotten quite that far) and arrived in South Braintree around noon. They had killed time in a speakeasy near South Braintree until the time of the robbery. After the robbery they switched to the Hudson car again in the Randolph woods near South Braintree, and the man who had brought the Buick drove it off separately again.[28]

Madeiros mentioned that a boy named Thomas Driver had seen the car driving through Randolph on the day of the crime. He himself had become acquainted with Driver several years later when he lived in Randolph with Weeks.[29]

Robert Montgomery argued that Madeiros's confession was an obvious falsehood and that he based his story of the South Braintree robbery on the Wrentham robbery he had perpetrated with Weeks, in which they had used a Buick and a Hudson car, and on what he had heard from the Drivers. Francis Russell has suggested that Madeiros told the story simply to prolong his life, although had this been his motive it would be hard to explain why he did not name any confederates. The main weakness in his story was his failure to remember any of the landmarks around Slater and Morrill—according to him, he sat in the back seat the whole time, half-drunk and too frightened to remember anything. His story does, however, tally with several other details of the crime that it would have been difficult if not impossible for him to have known.

Although if Madeiros was telling the truth he forgot one part of the story, most of his account of the gang's movements is corroborated by other evidence. Allowing a conservative two hours for the dawn trip from Providence to Andrews Square in South Boston, the gang would have arrived sometime after 6:00 A.M. The stop was apparently brief—Madeiros stayed in the car while a gang member went to get information. The men would have had about three hours to kill before showing up at South Braintree about 9:15, when they watched the delivery of the payroll to Slater and Morrill. Then they would have had another two hours to waste before they reappeared.

14. Mug shots of Nicola Sacco. (Courtesy Harvard Law School Library)

15. Mug shots of Joseph Morelli.
(Courtesy Harvard Law School Library)

16. Mug shot of William Dodson.
(Courtesy Harvard Law School Library)

Most interesting is Madeiros's hitherto ignored statement that the gang arrived back in South Braintree around noon. It is completely accurate. William Tracy testified at the trial that he saw two dark men standing in front of a drugstore at the corner of Pearl and Hancock streets, a block away from the railway tracks, at about 11:35 or 11:40. It was at roughly the same time that Lola Andrews and Julia Campbell saw the car with two men in and around it in front of Slater and Morrill. The railway policeman Heron saw two men in the train depot around 12:30. The presence of the car in front of the factory before noon suggests that the bandits were not sure when the payroll would be carried over and thought it might be just before lunch. But the car must have left the area not long after that, allowing for the trip to the nearby speakeasy to which Madeiros referred.

Indeed, no one sighted the car or anyone resembling the bandits again until about 2:20, when two suspicious characters entered the Braintree National Bank about two miles from where the shooting took place.[30] Ralph De Forrest saw two men and the Buick in front of the train depot at about 2:30; a few minutes later they had disappeared. This tallies almost perfectly with the evidence of a nurse, Jenny Novelli, who walked down Pearl Street almost alongside the car and saw it turn around in front of Slater and Morrill just before 3:00.[31] The shooting started a few minutes later. In short, the car and the bandits were seen in South Braintree on three separate occasions during the day: at about 9:30, between 11:30 and 12:30, and after 2:30. In between there was time for the trips to Rhode Island and the speakeasy that Madeiros described.

But the most sensational corroboration of Madeiros's statement related to his testimony that *two* cars had been used in the robbery. At the inquest two days after the South Braintree crime, Shelley Neal, the expressman who brought the payroll from the train station to the Slater and Morrill office at 9:30 A.M., said he had seen *two* strange cars outside the office. Neal, who had his hand in his pocket and his finger on the trigger of a pistol, heard a man in one car call "All right" to the other. Inside the door he found a thin blond man answering the description of the driver of the bandit car. When Neal came out he saw the blond man get into one of the cars, and the two cars drove off in opposite directions. Another man, Thomas Treacy, saw two cars in the same place at about the same time and recognized one of them in front of Slater and Morrill just before the shooting.[32] Press reports in the days immediately after the crime referred to this evidence and reported that the police believed the bandits had switched cars near South Braintree. Astonishingly, they added that the police suspected the bandits had escaped to Providence, the home of the Morellis.[33] But the evidence of a second car did not fit the prosecution's ultimate theory of the case. Neal changed his story at the trial so as to omit any mention of the second car, and Treacy was not called.[34] *Their testimony was unknown to the defense at the time of Madeiros's confession.* More than forty years later Herbert Ehrmann received a communication from Neal's brother Clifton informing him that Shelley Neal wanted to see him, but for various reasons Ehrmann failed to arrange a meeting until Neal had lost his memory. On 11 April 1966 Clifton Neal explained to him that his brother had always had a bad conscience over his failure to mention the second car in his trial testimony. He had wanted to do so, but Harold Williams, explaining that it would not fit with what else was known about the case, asked him to leave the second car out.[35]

The existence of a second car, combined with the evidence of some of the sightings of the bandit car after the robbery, calls the prosecution's theory of the movements of the would-be bandits on the day of the crime into serious question as well. Katzmann in his summary laid great stress on the finding of the bandit car in the Manley Woods less than two miles from Boda and Coacci's house. This, however, forced the prosecution to explain how Austin Reed, the gate tender at the Matfield crossing several miles *beyond* the Manley Woods, had sighted the car after four o'clock with five men in it. Williams in his opening statement suggested either that they had gotten lost or that they had intended to drive Vanzetti to Plymouth but changed their minds. On the surface these hypotheses seem plausible, especially since Reed saw the car return going westward a few minutes later, but they broke down in 1927 when an editor of the *Boston Evening Transcript*, James E. King, made a detailed study of the car's movements based on the reports of eyewitnesses. The study showed that the car could not have taken a full hour to get from South Braintree to Matfield unless it had been traveling at about fifteen miles an hour on the average, and every witness who saw it confirmed that it had been traveling at a fast rate of speed.[36] Madeiros's statement that the bandits had exchanged the Buick for a Hudson in Randolph, not far from South Braintree, explained the time lag in the getaway. The Randolph area was familiar to car thieves; the Randolph police chief deposed that two stolen Buicks had been abandoned there during the fall of 1920.[37]

Most extraordinary of all was what Ehrmann discovered in the police notebook of Sergeant Ellsworth Jacobs of the New Bedford police. Sev-

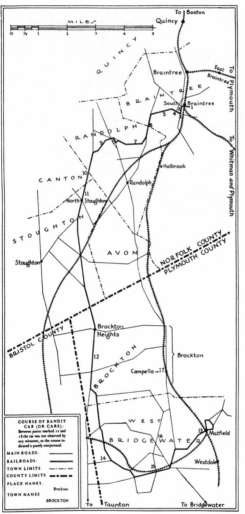

Approximate Time Table

SOUTH BRAINTREE

1. Pearl Street—place of crime, 3:05
2. Hancock Street—Chase—about 3:00
3. Plain Street crossing—Buckley, 3:10
4. Washington Street
5. Pond Street—Baker—about 3:00

RANDOLPH

6. North Street—Desmond, 3:12; Chisholm, 3:30
7. Oak Street—Farmer, 3:25
8. Orchard Street—Hewins
9. Chestnut Street, Tower Hill

CANTON

10. Turnpike—Dorr, 3:30; Lloyd, 3:30

STOUGHTON

11. Turnpike—Clark, 3:45

BROCKTON

12. Pearl Street—Kelliher, 3:50
17. Campello—place of arrest

WEST BRIDGEWATER

14. Manley Woods—where Buick car was found
15. Johnson house, North Elm Street
16. North Elm Street trolley

MATFIELD

13. Crossing—Reed, 4:15

17. The path of the bandit car. (Reprinted, by permission, from Fraenkel, *Sacco-Vanzetti Case.* © 1931 by Alfred A. Knopf, Inc. © 1959 by Osmond K. Fraenkel)

18. The Manley Woods, where the bandit car was found on 17 April 1920. (Courtesy Boston Public Library)

eral days before the robbery Jacobs had seen Mike Morelli, who was well known to him as a member of the gang, driving a Buick touring car with a Rhode Island license plate. He had seen the same automobile again at about 5:30 in the afternoon on 15 April. Eight days later he saw the same license plate on a Cole car in front of a restaurant. Inside he found four nervous men, including Frank ("Butsey") Morelli. Morelli said he was in the automobile business and switched the plate himself.[38] Jacobs added that he had suspected the Morellis of the South Braintree crime. Madeiros had stated that another Italian had met the gang with the Buick in Randolph on the morning of 15 April and driven it away in the afternoon after the shooting with the intention of leaving it in the woods elsewhere. Jacobs's story tallied with this perfectly; if Mike reclaimed the Buick immediately after the robbery he could easily have reached New Bedford by 5:30. It would also have made sense to have put a Massachusetts plate on the Buick for the few hours between the two meetings in the Randolph woods, replacing the Rhode Island plate after Mike reclaimed the car a few minutes after the shooting. If he dumped the Buick in the Manley Woods the next night, it would explain why it was not found until the morning of 17 April, even though the Manley Woods was a popular area for horseback riders.[39] The presence of the license plate on a Cole 8 a few days later is also easily explained; the car in the Manley Woods was found without a plate. The *Boston Post* of 18 April reported that tracks of another car led out of the Manley Woods where the Buick was found, also militating against the prosecution's theory that Boda or Coacci had left the car in the woods on 15 April and walked home.[40]

Neglected eyewitness testimony also supports the theory that the bandits switched their cars in Randolph rather than in the Manley Woods. Pelser, the only trial witness who testified to having gotten the number plate of the car in South Braintree, testified that the plate was on the *front* of the car. Several other witnesses confirmed that there had been no number plate on the back of the car.[41] Yet two witnesses who saw the car between Randolph and Bridgewater—Francis Clark, who was driving a bakery wagon in North Stoughton, and Julia Kelliher, a schoolgirl walking home in Brockton—testified specifically that they saw the number *on the back* of the car. On cross-examination McAnarney brought out that in January 1921 Clark had told Defense Attorney Callahan that he though the car was "either a Buick or a Hudson."[42]

Both Thayer and the Supreme Judicial Court denied another motion for a new trial based on Madeiros's confession and the related evidence, and Governor Fuller and the Lowell Committee refused to give the new evidence any weight. Still, the Morelli question became cloudier and cloudier after Sacco and Vanzetti's execution. During the 1930s Joe Morelli began peddling his autobiography, a mysterious manuscript that he claimed would reveal the truth about South Braintree and other details of an extraordinary life of crime. As he refused to show it to anyone without a large advance payment, no outsider was ever allowed to read it. In 1950, after serving another stretch in jail, he was released, critically ill. Through an intermediary a *Providence Journal* reporter, Ben Bagdikian, received an invitation to see Joe and hear the whole story at last, but when Bagdikian arrived Morelli had lapsed into a coma from which he never emerged.[43]

In 1961 Francis Russell apparently obtained some form of access to Joe's manuscript and subsequently provided a summary of its contents to Herbert Ehrmann. The summary states that Joe knew Sacco and Vanzetti, that they had planned the holdup together, that he had been to South Braintree to case it, but that they had double-crossed him and pulled the job a week early with Boda, Orciani, and Coacci. It added that Coacci had helped Joe steal shoes from Slater and Morrill and that Berardelli was also his confederate.[44] Ehrmann argued that Joe's story was typical of several past attempts to throw his own misdeeds—including the 1920 freight-car robberies—on his confederates. Nor was it accidental that he duplicated the prosecution theory of the crime; Ben Bagdikian found that Morelli had read a copy of Osmond K. Fraenkel's exhaustive study, *The Sacco-Vanzetti Case*, while preparing his manuscript. One could conclude that this story was true only if Morelli provided previously unknown but verifiable information about the anarchists he claimed to know, information he could not have secured from published sources. Russell, however, did not address this point.

Morelli's autobiography is not presently available for inspection. It may possibly contain some detail that might be corroborated and thereby provide a real new insight into the crime. It might in particular shed light on Berardelli's role and corroborate the testimony of his wife and neighbor regarding his nervousness on the day of the crime. In the present state of our knowledge, however, this is only speculation.

More provocative yet is an admission from Frank Morelli reported by Mafia informant Vincent Teresa in his 1975 autobiography, *My Life in the Mafia*. A longtime underworld figure, Teresa had become acquainted with Joe Morelli's younger brother Frank, who had eventually eclipsed his older sibling and become the organized-crime boss of New England. In the midst of his reminiscences of a long life of crime, Teresa recalled that during the 1950s Frank ("Butsey") Morelli, then critically ill with cancer, had sued the *Boston Globe* after it printed a story accusing the Morellis of the South Braintree murders. Morelli was angry because the story had brought these accusations to the attention of his adopted son, who was largely ignorant of his father's past. Teresa asked Morelli why he was suing.

> I asked him, "What the hell are you suing them for? You can't beat a newspaper." He said: "They're implicating me in this Sacco-Vanzetti thing. What they said was true, but it's going to hurt my kid. I don't give a damn about myself. I'm ready to die anyway. But look what they're doing to my boy. He's a legitimate kid. He never knew what was going on before."
>
> I looked at Butsey. I didn't know much about the case except what I'd heard. But he was upset because of what was happening to his boy, not what happened to Sacco and Vanzetti. "We whacked them out, we killed those guys in the robbery," Butsey said. "These two greaseballs [Sacco and Vanzetti] took it on the chin. They got in our way so we just ran over them. Now after all

these years some punch-drunk writer has got to start up the whole thing over again—ruin my reputation. . . ." I said: "Did you really do this?" He looked at me, right into my eyes, and said: "Absolutely, Vinnie. Those two suckers took it on the chin for us. That shows you how much justice there really is."[45]

The evidence against the Morellis is largely circumstantial. It is possible that Madeiros, who clearly intended to implicate them even though he never used their names, did so for reasons of his own. Madeiros might actually have committed the South Braintree crime with a group of his own friends. Steve Benkovsky, whose picture was identified by some witnesses as a likeness of the driver of the bandit car, was an associate of Madeiros rather than of the Morelli gang. Another suspect is James Weeks, who was sentenced to life imprisonment for the Wrentham robbery for which Madeiros was executed. Many years after the crime Joe Sammarco, a fellow inmate of all these men, said that he had suspected Weeks of committing the South Braintree crime and the Bridgewater holdup, and another former inmate, Francis Moriarity, has recently stated that it was "common knowledge" in Charlestown State Prison that Weeks had done the South Braintree job. Herbert Ehrmann, who maintained an acquaintance with Weeks after Weeks's eventual release from prison, also suspected Weeks of participating.[46]

Madeiros's confession is in any case very hard to explain away. No one has ever satisfactorily explained how he could have known about the two cars, the switch in the Randolph woods, and the movements of the gang unless he himself was involved in the crime. The confession is not proof, but it is an important factor that must be weighed in any analysis of the guilt of Sacco and Vanzetti.

In recent years, Francis Russell has also made much of comments from two persons close to the defense—Fred Moore, the attorney, and the anarchist Carlo Tresca—suggesting that either Sacco or Vanzetti might have been guilty. The background to these statements, however, suggests that they must be regarded with extreme caution.

We have seen that after their arrest Sacco and Vanzetti originally employed two local lawyers, John Vahey and John Graham. The shock of Vanzetti's extraordinary twelve-to-fifteen-year sentence in Plymouth persuaded his friends to look elsewhere for help. The printer

Aldino Felicani, a friend of Vanzetti's, contacted the anarchist leader Carlo Tresca in New York to ask for help. Eight years earlier Tresca had been involved in another Massachusetts murder case, the trial of Joe Ettor and Arturo Giovanetti for a killing during the famous Lawrence mill strike of 1912. The strike had been organized by the IWW and an IWW lawyer, Fred Moore, had helped prepare the case. The men had been acquitted. Now Tresca suggested that Moore return to Massachusetts and take over the defense of Sacco and Vanzetti.

It was a fateful decision. A man of considerable intelligence and great energy, Moore threw himself wholeheartedly into the case. It was he who turned it into a national and international cause célèbre and tapped the funds of radical groups and unions around the country to help the two men. In addition, his investigators, led by Robert Reid, undertook a massive pretrial investigation of the case, making every effort to interview every possible witness. Yet from the beginning his personal relations with the anarchists who ran the defense committee and with Sacco were strained, and he apparently made an unfortunate impression in the Dedham courtroom. In the months before the trial he insisted that the two men could not get a fair trial in Norfolk County, a refrain that may have become a self-fulfilling prophecy. He explicitly indicted Massachusetts justice by his handling of the De Falco incident, which as we have seen obviously rebounded upon his two clients. His flamboyant life style and insatiable demands for money immediately created difficulties with his Italian anarchist employers, including Sacco and Rosina Sacco. No one ever accused him of profiting from his defense of Sacco and Vanzetti, but he constantly requested more funds for investigations; nothing the committee raised ever seemed to be enough.[47]

Moore intended to try the case in court, but in the spring of 1921 he apparently decided to engage a local lawyer as well. He approached the three McAnarney brothers—John W., Thomas F., and Jeremiah J. ("Jerry")—a well-known Norfolk County firm that handled many serious Southeastern Distict criminal cases. As John W. McAnarney explained to the Lowell Committee in 1927, because of the nature of the crime he and his brothers did not want the case unless they were certain of their clients' innocence. After long talks with Sacco and his wife, with Moore, and with Vanzetti, they were persuaded that these men had not committed the South Braintree crime.[48] They never changed their minds.

At the beginning of the trial Moore concentrated on establishing some procedural irregularity that would enable him to reverse a conviction on appeal. In the first days he questioned the way in which potential jurors had been summoned and submitted to Judge Thayer, who under the law had the sole power of interrogating them, a list of questions for the jurors, including their attitudes toward organized labor. Moore, whose manner, clothes, and accent immediately marked him as an outsider, aroused the obvious antagonism of Thayer. During jury selection Moore also dismayed Thomas McAnarney by insisting on excluding two men because they worked for a brokerage house and a trust company. He apparently wanted only workingmen to sit on the case.[49]

Two days of these preliminaries were sufficient to drive Jerry and Thomas McAnarney to despair. They informed their brother John that the antagonism between Thayer and Moore made Moore's withdrawal from the case essential, a view shared by Mrs. Sacco. John McAnarney called William G. Thompson, one of the most prominent trial lawyers in Boston, and asked him to come to Dedham the same day. When Thompson arrived the McAnarneys made a desperate attempt to persuade Moore to withdraw from the case and to persuade Thompson to take it over. But both men refused, Moore because he was too proud to surrender the reins and Thompson because he felt, rightly, that he could not possibly take over a murder trial with no opportunity for preparation. Still, a few minutes in the courtroom did persuade Thompson of the seriousness of the McAnarneys' predicament. Thayer, he told them, was determined to convict the two men but clever enough to keep his prejudice out of the written record so as to prevent a reversal.[50] Moore seems to have realized that he had become a liability as the trial went on, and he left more and more of the direct and cross-examination to Jerry McAnarney and another local lawyer, William J. Callahan, in its later stages. Several years later a juror told Thompson that he thought the jury had shared Thayer's opinion of Moore.

As we look at it today, the conduct of the Dedham defense seems erratic. The defense had prepared its case diligently and was particularly skillful in finding witnesses to refute key prosecution testimony. Yet the defense attorneys also indulged in a great deal of aimless cross-examination. Witnesses who had merely seen the getaway car without identifying the defendants were sometimes grilled as if it were vital to discredit them. At times jurors must have wondered whether the defense was really trying to prove that no murder had taken place at all. Their worst mistake involved their handling of the prosecution's firearms experts. From the record, the prosecutors—and particularly Katzmann—seem somewhat more sure of their case. Whether other attorneys could have done better will never be known.

After the trial Moore seems to have spent most of his time and money trying to discredit prosecution witnesses like Goodridge, Andrews, and Pelser and investigating rumors that other criminals had confessed to the Bridgewater and South Braintree crimes.[51] After numerous quarrels with the defense committee over money he formed a committee of his own to raise funds. For Sacco this was the last straw; in August 1924 he fired Moore. Moore left Boston broke and embittered.

In 1953, many years after Moore's death, Upton Sinclair, who had thoroughly researched the case for his novel *Boston*, described a conversation with Moore not long after the execution of Sacco and Vanzetti. "He had come reluctantly to the conclusion," Sinclair wrote, "that Sacco was guilty of the crime for which he had died and that possibly Vanzetti also was guilty." Neither the defendants nor any of their friends had ever told Moore this, but Moore said that "some of the anarchists were then raising funds for their movement by robbery. It was strictly honest from the group's point of view—that is to say, they kept none of the money for themselves." Moore added that he had once given a ride from New York to Boston to two anarchists wanted for robbery at the behest of anarchist leader Carlo Tresca. Sinclair subsequently spoke to Moore's ex-wife Lola, who confessed her astonishment, added that Moore had never made such a remark to her in all the years that they worked together on the case, and concluded, "I feel that Fred is embittered because he was dropped from the case, and it has poisoned his mind." It may also have been during this conversation that Moore discussed the perjury committed by Sacco's alibi witness, James Hayes. "Fred was a criminal lawyer," Sinclair wrote, "and I remember one of his statements about his profession. He said, 'There is no criminal lawyer who has attained to fame in America except by inventing alibis and hiring witnesses. There is no other way to be a great criminal lawyer in America.' "[52] In his account Sinclair's memory failed him on some minor points, but Moore undoubtedly made some such statement. It cannot, however, be regarded as clear evidence; even Moore admitted that he had no proof.

In recent years the statements of another man connected with the case have also attracted enormous attention: Carlo Tresca, a leading Italian-American anarchist and the man who brought Moore into the defense. More than twenty years ago Max Eastman, a former Communist, wrote that in 1942, a few weeks before Tresca's death, Tresca told him that Sacco was guilty but that Vanzetti was not. Subsequent research showed that Tresca had made similar remarks to the American Socialist leader, Norman Thomas, and to John Roche, now a prominent political scientist and at one time chairman of Americans for Democratic Action. These statements have been taken by some as irrefutable proof that Sacco was guilty—particularly those like Francis Russell who identify Tresca as the acknowledged leader of all Italian-American anarchists.[53]

Tempting though it may be to regard Tresca's statement as the Rosetta stone of the case, the historian Nunzio Pernicone has shown this finding to be hasty.[54] While there is no doubt that Tresca made these statements, evidence of his beliefs at other times and his real relationship to the defendants and the case suggests that they cannot be regarded as unimpeachable truth. Galleani, not Tresca, was the leader of the extreme faction to which Sacco and Vanzetti belonged, and Tresca's name almost never appears in the numerous Bureau of Investigation files on Galleani and his followers. The Galleanisti's violent rejection of all forms of authority brought them into conflict with the anarcho-syndicalist Tresca both before and after the case. Unlike the Galleanisti, Tresca did not believe in direct action and terrorism, a fact that makes Moore's story of giving two anarchist bandits a lift, as reported by Sinclair, somewhat difficult to believe. Furthermore, Tresca was not at all involved with Sacco and Vanzetti's defense before Vanzetti's Plymouth conviction, and even after he brought Moore into the case he seems to have taken relatively little interest in it. During the fall of 1920, while Moore was preparing the defense, Moore frequently asked Tresca for information and favors in connection with the case, while gently hinting that the "local committee"—dominated by Galleanisti—did not think that Tresca was giving the case enough publicity. On 9 December 1920 Tresca wired Moore, "Decided to have nothing more to do except speaking when and where requested so don't ask me for things to do please." The correspondence faded out rapidly after that.[55]

Nor was this all. The secretary of the defense committee, Emilio Coda, hated Tresca and conducted public polemics against him beginning in 1925. Furthermore, throughout the 1920s Tresca expressed his belief in the two men's *innocence* both to his closest anarchist associates and to his own daughter. Pernicone concludes that Tresca's subsequent remarks probably owed something to a long polemic the

Galleanisti had conducted against him from 1925 through 1938; Tresca seems to have been venting his rage against his fellow Italian-Americans to selected left-wing Americans.[56] Since Tresca was never close to Sacco and Vanzetti before the crime or to other Galleanisti subsequently, it seems unlikely that any participant in the crime could have confessed to him. His most likely source was Moore, whom he had known for many years. Moore's doubts reflected his own guilt and frustration; Tresca's, his ambivalence about the defendants. Their statements do not prove Sacco and Vanzetti's guilt any more than Madeiros's confession or Frank Morelli's reported statements prove their innocence.

13 / Conclusion

Any attempt to establish the guilt or innocence of Sacco and Vanzetti must be based upon an analysis of the evidence against them. Both the principles of Anglo-American jurisprudence and the logic of historical inquiry compel us to declare them innocent in the absence of any convincing proof of their guilt. The vast documentation now available has enabled us to tell the story of the preparation of the prosecution's case in almost all its aspects. The revelations of the state police files, the grand jury proceeding, and the prosecution notebooks show that virtually every piece of evidence against the two men ultimately rested upon falsehoods and fabrications. The authors of this book have attempted to avoid psychological speculation and base their conclusions on concrete evidence to the maximum extent possible, but some explanation of the prosecution's conduct is clearly called for. It is impossible to know what went on inside the minds of Stewart, Brouillard, Katzmann, and Williams, but evidence leaves room for some hypotheses regarding their motives.

In May 1920 southeastern Massachusetts was preoccupied with three recent holdups: the successful stickup of the Randolph Savings Bank in November 1919, the attempted robbery of the L. Q. White payroll in December, and the double murder and fifteen-thousand-dollar robbery in South Braintree. The United States was also passing through a period of extreme patriotism and nativism, and local opinion, as reflected in newspaper comment, also viewed the growth of radical agitation with considerable alarm. In Boston a local legislator had introduced a resolution calling for a substantial reward to anyone who could find the perpetrators of the three holdups. In late April Chief Michael Stewart of Bridgewater stumbled upon a small group of anarchists and quickly concluded that he had found the Bridgewater and South Braintree bandits. After the arrests of Sacco, Vanzetti, and Orciani his conclusions were immediately endorsed by the district attorney's office.

Despite the failure of most of the witnesses to identify either bandit and despite the initial lack of any physical evidence, the district attorney's office was saying within a few days that it was certain it had found the men it was after. Prejudice seems to have played some role in Stewart's conclusions. His initial comments on the Bridgewater holdup reflect his deeply held suspicions of Reds, Bolsheviks, and anarchists, and he has been frequently quoted as saying after the discovery of the South Braintree bandit car that "the men who did this job knew no God."[1] His prejudices meshed with his understandable desire to bring in the perpetrators of a sensational robbery and murder. "He has the reputation of an energetic convictor," a defense investigator noted during the preparation of the trial after talking to other police officers. "In this case he is said to be obsessed with the desire to get somebody and he has been ceaseless in his efforts."[2]

Stewart was a small-town policeman with little experience and few investigative resources and a man for whom professionals had little respect. The chief of the Brockton Police Department—a much larger operation—refused to detail any of his men to assist Stewart's investigation.[3] Virtually nothing is known about Albert Brouillard, the state police officer who assisted Stewart in his investigation, although an undated note among the defense papers describes him as a graduate of reform school.[4] The Norfolk County district attorney's office nonetheless accepted Stewart's conclusions. Their motives are equally difficult to fathom, but some evidence does suggest that they too had strong antiradical feelings. Thus Katzmann and William Kane had brought the case against Sergis Zakoff for advocating anarchy in April of 1920, and Katzmann certainly made a determined attempt to inflame the jury in regard to Sacco and Vanzetti's radical views during his cross-examination of them in Dedham.[5] In addition, during the First World War, George Adams, the assistant district attorney who conducted the preliminary hearings against the two men, served as Norfolk County chairman of the recruiting committee of the Massachusetts Committee of Public Safety. According to the official history of the committee, the recruiting committee had the responsibility of meeting the threat posed by "pacifists, anarchists, slackers and hyphenated Americans" by insuring that in recruiting "neither the birth, character nor antecedents of the would-be soldier should be open to slightest suspicion."[6]

Although in July 1920 the prosecution secured the conviction of Vanzetti for the Bridgewater holdup, some indications do suggest that by the fall of 1920 the prosecution was having second thoughts about the case. In the grand jury proceeding Katzmann secured murder indictments of both men, but he clearly realized how little evidence he really had. The identification witnesses he relied upon could not have inspired him with confidence. Several of them gave positive identifications only after considerable prompting, while one or two others told stories with major discrepancies. No trial date was set for more than three months. In January, Mrs. De Falco's approach signaled the defense that the prosecution might be willing to make some sort of deal.

Fred Moore's decision to make Mrs. De Falco's offer public eliminated any possibility of a plea bargain. The prosecution had no choice but to proceed with the case. It was at this time that William Kane, the assistant district attorney who had presented the Commonwealth's case at Vanzetti's Plymouth trial, seems to have left the case, to be replaced by Harold Williams. Several months later Kane made an extraordinary remark to an eyewitness to the South Braintree crime, a Brockton police officer named Harry Schwartz. As Schwartz explained to Stewart on 19 May 1921, he had been unable to identify Sacco as a man he had seen leaning out of the getaway car and firing in South Braintree. "I have never given any statement to the other side but have been asked for one several times," Schwartz continued. "I went to the District Attorney's office to ask for advice as to whether I should talk or not and talked with Assistant District Attorney Kane. He told me that he didn't care who I talked to, that he wasn't interested."[7] For reasons we can never know, Kane apparently wanted nothing more to do with the case of Sacco and Vanzetti.

Williams does not seem to have taken long to realize that something was rotten in the prosecution's case. One of his loose-leaf notebooks, prepared in the first months of 1921, contains a brief outline of the Bridgewater and Braintree cases. The outline, which may have been prepared to help argue appeals of Vanzetti's Plymouth conviction, begins with a quick chronology of the key dates of the two crimes and a summary of the state's evidence against Vanzetti. The next two pages deserve to be reproduced in full.

> 3
> Why the Verdict
> (a) – Prejudice against Stations
> (b) – " " Reds
> (c) – Failure to prepare case.
> (d) – " " put Defendant on stand.
> (e) – " " secure necessary witnesses.
> 5
> Elements of Frame-up
> a – Proctor description given to newspapers

    b – Witnesses all bear marks of coaching
    Bowles
    Cox
    c – Hat matter
    d – Cap Matter
    e – Salsedo-Elia
    f – Johnson-rew——
    Stewart –
    g – Defendants State ———
    to May 5 ———
    h – Police story that trap ready to spring
    i – Bullets.

Of this list, 5a presumably refers to the original descriptions of the bandits released to the newspapers, which did not fit Sacco and Vanzetti. The notation 5b is self-explanatory; 5c is less so. The 5d entry could refer to the cap turned in by Fred Loring and later argued to be Sacco's, but it probably refers instead to a cap police found in Vanzetti's lodgings which the prosecution tried to have a Bridgewater eyewitness identify as having belonged to one of the Bridgewater bandits. The notation of 5e indicates considerable prosecution knowledge of the defendants' radical connections—probably furnished by the Bureau of Investigation—and seems to indicate that the prosecution understood the real reasons for the defendants' behavior at the time of their arrest. Of the remaining entries 5f seems to refer to a reward paid to Simon Johnson, and perhaps also to Stewart; 5g is inexplicable; 5h seems to suggest that the whole story of Stewart's having asked Simon Johnson to call him if Boda ever came for his car was not true; the significance of 5i is left to the reader's speculation.

Despite his obvious awareness that all was not well with the case, Williams went ahead with its preparation. In all probability he persuaded himself at some point in the proceedings that the two men were guilty; indeed, it is unlikely that any prosecutor ever undertakes a case without satisfying himself of the justice of his cause. Still, the ways in which Williams handled the testimony of many of his witnesses so as to cover up the inconsistencies in the prosecution's case are striking. Knowing that the eyewitness William Heron had initially told police that the two men he claimed to have seen in South Braintree at midday on 15 April were smoking, Williams induced him to say on the stand that the one he identified as the nonsmoker Sacco was not smoking. He

induced James Bostock to say that he had seen Berardelli with his revolver a few days before the shooting when in fact, as Bostock admitted
on cross-examination, he had only seen Berardelli's revolver once,
months earlier. He put forward the claim that Vanzetti's revolver had
been taken from Berardelli, even though he must have known that this
was not so, and omitted the claim from his opening statement so as
to give the defense less time to discover the truth. Although he was
familiar with Officer Connelly's grand jury testimony, in which Connelly had described the routine arrest of Sacco and Vanzetti, he allowed
him to tell a completely different story on the stand. And knowing that
Dr. Magrath believed the four Berardelli bullets had come from the
same weapon, he induced him to say that he did not know what kind of
gun had fired bullet III and prevented him from looking at the four bullets simultaneously on the stand. Indeed, there is evidence that his
conscience was not altogether clear. At the conclusion of the trial,
about ten minutes after the verdict had been read, a defense attorney approached him and, following legal etiquette, offered him congratula-
tions on a brilliant victory. "For God's sake," replied Williams, "don't
rub it in. This is the saddest day of my life."[8]

Katzmann's involvement in the preparation of the evidence is harder
to establish. He did not present the Commonwealth's case, and when
questioned by Thompson about certain aspects of the case before the
Lowell Committee he repeatedly denied any responsibility for its
preparation. In subsequent years Katzmann refused to discuss the case
in public. One interesting footnote regarding his attitude and involvement comes from the recently released state police files. In 1950 the
state police received a letter from a researcher asking for copies of photographs of the ballistics evidence in the case taken by Van Amburgh.
The researcher added that he hoped to show beyond a doubt that Sacco
and Vanzetti were guilty. The state police referred the question to
Edmund Dewing, the district attorney for the Southeastern District,
who in turn contacted Katzmann. Katzmann asked that no material be
released, and none was.[9]

Whether the conduct of Katzmann and Williams in the case was un-
usually duplicitous, unprofessional, or criminal is a question only professional attorneys could answer. Having decided to prosecute the case,
they took advantage of every opportunity to strengthen it. If nothing
else, their behavior underlines the appropriateness—if not, indeed, the
necessity—of several important Warren Court decisions regarding the
rights of defendants. Most notable among these is the rule that prosecu-

tors must disclose all exculpatory material, a requirement that would have forced the prosecution to reveal the truth about Berardelli's revolver and to reveal Connelly's grand jury testimony.

If a frame consists of the conscious fabrication of evidence, there is no question that Sacco and Vanzetti were framed. Yet is there room for doubt as to their innocence or guilt?

With respect to Vanzetti, the new information with respect to Berardelli's revolver removes the only significant piece of evidence against him. The identification evidence against him is shaky in the extreme, all the more so since his long, flowing mustache would surely have impressed itself upon more of the onlookers had he been present. Officer Connelly's grand jury testimony shows that he did not try to draw his gun when informed he was under arrest. The most incriminating piece of evidence against him is his association with Sacco. It was evidently upon these grounds that the Lowell Committee decided he should be electrocuted; a letter of Lowell's written after the committee's decision reported its conclusion that Vanzetti had been the planner and Sacco an executioner of the crime.[10]

Such a conclusion, while *legally* appalling in the absence of any evidence for it, is not without some shred of plausibility if one presumes Sacco guilty. And if bullet III is genuine Sacco is probably guilty. It is possible that someone else used his gun, but the coincidence of his absence from work on 15 April would make this hypothesis doubtful.

No single piece of evidence definitely confirms that bullet III was a substitute. The scratches on the bottom of bullet III are sufficiently similar to those on the others to have been made by the same instrument. The evidence of the eyewitnesses and autopsies does indicate that bullet III could not have been fired from a different weapon, but such evidence is not absolutely infallible. The grand jury proceeding suggests that in September 1920 all four bullets did in fact show similar markings, but because Proctor did not testify and because the state of Magrath's knowledge of firearms is unknown, we cannot be sure. The most powerful evidence in favor of a switch is Williams's notes relating to the shells found upon the ground, which suggest that Shay originally found only three of them. Williams's handling of the identification of the bullets by Magrath also indicates that he doubted the authenticity of bullet III. Together these facts point very strongly toward a switch.

The question of a possible substitution, moreover, must not be considered in isolation. To believe that bullet III and shell W are genuine, not only must one disregard the direct evidence that they were not, one must also explain away the extraordinary weakness of the rest of the prosecution's case. Why, if Sacco was guilty, did the best eyewitnesses fail to identify him? Why was the prosecution unable to make any convincing case as to the identity of the other bandits or to trace any of the stolen money? How is Madeiros's knowledge of the crime to be explained? Who drove the Buick? Where did the second car come from? What did the anarchists want the money for, and what did they do with it?

To believe that bullet III is genuine, one must not only explain away all the evidence that it could not in fact have been fired from a different gun than the others, one must also believe that, despite the transparency of all the rest of the evidence against Sacco and Vanzetti, the prosecution, almost by accident, had stumbled upon one real bandit. This may be conceivable; it is hardly likely. The case is destined to remain controversial, but the truth should not be in doubt. The overwhelming probability is that a substitution of bullets did take place and that Sacco and Vanzetti were completely innocent of the South Braintree murders.

Notes

Chapter 1

1. *The Sacco-Vanzetti Case: Transcript of the Record of the Trial of Nicola Sacco and Bartolomeo Vanzetti in the Courts of Massachusetts and Subsequent Proceedings, 1920–7,* 5 vols., with a supplemental volume (New York: Henry Holt, 1928).

Chapter 2

1. See Roberta Strauss Feuerlicht, *Justice Crucified* (New York: McGraw-Hill, 1977), and the most inadequate treatment by Brian Jackson, *The Black Flag* (Boston: Routledge and Kegan Paul, 1981).

2. See below, chap. 11.

3. *The Sacco-Vanzetti Case,* 3:3580.

4. David M. Kennedy, *Over Here: The First World War and American Society* (New York: Oxford University Press, 1980), pp. 45–92.

5. Arthur S. Link, ed., *The Papers of Woodrow Wilson,* vol. 35 (Princeton: Princeton University Press, 1980), pp. 306–7.

6. H. C. Peterson and Gilbert C. Fite, *Opponents of War, 1917–18* (Madison: University of Wisconsin Press, 1957), pp. 15–17, 215–21.

7. Typical reports from Boston began with a table of information on strikes and labor disputes, including the affected industry, the number of workers involved, their nationality, and the issues in the dispute. Then followed lengthy reports on the activities of local Communists, Socialists, anarchists, iww members, and any and all individuals or groups displaying any sympathy for these ideologies or their adherents. The weekly Boston reports will be found in the National Archives, Record Group 65 (hereafter omitted), Bureau Series (hereafter BS) 202600-22. See also David Williams, "The Bureau of Investigation and Its Critics, 1919–1921: The Origins of Federal Political Surveillance," *Journal of American History* 68, no. 3 (December 1981): 560–79.

8. Joan M. Jensen, *The Price of Vigilance* (Chicago: Rand McNally, 1968).

9. See William Preston, Jr., *Aliens and Dissenters: Federal Suppression of Radicals, 1903–33* (New York: Harper Torchbook edition, 1966), pp. 82–83, 181–83.

10. Melvyn Dubofsky, *We Shall Be All: A History of the Industrial Workers of the World* (Chicago:

Quadrangle Press, 1969), pp. 349–407.

11. James Weinstein, *The Decline of Socialism in America, 1912–25* (New York: Monthly Review Press, 1967), pp. 93–176; Peterson and Fite, *Opponents of War*, pp. 43–49, 157–66, 248–55.

12. See Galleani deportation file, U.S. Immigration and Naturalization Service (hereafter INS), file 54235/33.

13. Ibid.; Nunzio Pernicone, "Carlo Tresca and the Sacco-Vanzetti Case," *Journal of American History* 66, no. 3 (December 1979): 535–47; Robert D'Attilio, "La Salute è in Voi: The Anarchist Dimension," in *Sacco-Vanzetti: Developments and Reconsiderations, 1979*, Boston, 1982 (conference proceedings).

14. Ryder memorandum, 23 July 1917, and Caminetti to Ryder, 23 August 1917, Galleani deportation file.

15. The 1917 list has not survived in the files, but a subsequent subscription list included both their addresses as of 1917, before their departure for Mexico. See report of William West, 7 October 1919, Department of Justice file 9-12-276, National Archives.

16. Agent Flynn's report, 27 March 1918, BI, OG 20713. The Bureau of Investigation's (BI) Old German (OG) files are on microfilm at the National Archives.

17. Commissioner General to Acting Secretary, 8 May 1918, INS file 54235/33.

18. Assistant Commissioner General of Immigration to J. Edgar Hoover, 7 May 1920, BI, OG 20713. For unexplained reasons, Brini was never apprehended or questioned.

19. Commissioner General of Immigration to Boston Commissioner, 13 May 1918, INS file 54779/351, includes the list of New England area suspects.

20. Memorandum by M. E. Stewart, 31 May 1921, Massachusetts State Police files.

21. INS file 54235/33.

22. Weiss reports, 8 September and 24 October 1919, BS 211793.

23. McDevitt report, 22 September 1919, BS 211793.

24. *General and Special Acts and Resolves Passed by the Legislature of Massachusetts during the Session of 1919* (Boston, n.d.), p. 115.

25. *Boston Herald*, 23 May 1919.

26. See the *Brockton Times*, 31 October 1919.

27. Newspaper clipping (unidentified), 14 January 1921, in Fred Moore Papers, book 1, Boston Public Library (BPL).

28. See informant's reports of 20 and 24 December 1919, and Becker to Hoover, 9 March 1920, BS 211793. The Massachusetts Department of Public Safety reports that it has no surviving

records of any bombing investigations, however, and a search of the Calvin Coolidge Papers in the Massachusetts Statehouse Library has also yielded no result.

29. See the Pinkerton reports of 24 December and 30 December 1919, in *The Sacco-Vanzetti Case*, supp. vol., pp. 367, 382, 391.

30. Hoover to Flynn, 8 March 1920, BS 211793; see also memorandum by Agent Drew, 14 May 1920, ibid.

31. Memorandum by John Creighton, 17 May 1920, BS 211793. The full file on the two men's arrest, including their interrogations, will be found in FBI file 61-260; see especially serials 38 and 54. (FBI series 61 files were obtained by the authors under the Freedom of Information Act.)

32. John A. Dowd to Hoover, 1 October 1926, FBI file 61-126-721. No copy of the interrogation has survived.

33. *The Sacco-Vanzetti Case*, 2:2006.

34. Davis report, 25 March 1920, BS 211793. Sacco's grandson Spencer Sacco of Newport, Rhode Island, has informed me that Assunta Valdinocci stayed with his family for years.

35. *Dedham Transcript*, 10 April 1920.

36. *Boston Globe*, 24 April 1920, morning ed.; *Boston Herald*, 24 April 1920; *Norwood Messenger*, 1 May 1920.

37. *Boston Globe*, 20 April evening ed. and 21 April morning ed., 1920.

38. See below, chap. 12.

39. FBI agents insisted after Salsedo's death that he had never been mistreated. See FBI files 61-260-151 through 61-260-157, and file 62-18674. Elia, on the other hand, later swore an affidavit that Salsedo had been tortured (*The Sacco-Vanzetti Case*, 5:4983–87).

40. *New York Times*, 4 May 1920; *Boston Globe*, 4 May 1920; *Boston Herald*, 4 May 1920.

41. For Stewart's account of these happenings, see the memorandum by M. E. Stewart, 31 May 1921, Massachusetts State Police files.

42. Thus reports stated not only that Sacco had missed work on 15 April, which was true, but that he had missed the following few days as well, which was not. Authorities claimed that many witnesses had seen the missing "fourth man" (clearly Boda, who was never apprehended) driving the bandit car in West Bridgewater; this also turned out to be a gross exaggeration. Other stories that several people had seen the bandits alighting from the car in West Bridgewater on the afternoon of the crime also later proved false.

43. *Boston Globe*, 7–9 May 1920, morning and evening eds.; *Brockton Times*, 8 May 1920.

44. Fred J. Cook, "The Missing

Fingerprints," *Nation*, 22 December 1962.

45. Thus, at the trial of Sacco and Vanzetti he was heard to say, "These are not the right men. Oh no, you haven't got the right men" (*The Sacco-Vanzetti Case*, 5: 5055). According to William G. Thompson, Proctor said in 1923 that he had given Katzmann his opinion of the two men's innocence before the Dedham trial (p. 4539).

Chapter 3

1. This decision later became the subject of endless recriminations between Vanzetti and his attorneys. Especially bitter because Vahey had become Katzmann's law partner, Vanzetti claimed that it was on his attorney's advice that he had remained silent. It seems, however, that he was partly to blame as well, particularly since he apparently refused to tell the truth about the reasons for his presence in Bridgewater on 5 May and about his visit to the Johnson garage. Lies on these subjects would undoubtedly have made a poor impression.

2. See Elizabeth F. Loftus, *Eyewitness Testimony* (Cambridge: Harvard University Press, 1979), an authoritative work based on numerous experiments.

3. Pinkerton report, 24 December 1919, in *The Sacco-Vanzetti Case*, supp. vol., pp. 364–67.

4. Pinkerton reports, 26, 27, and 29 December 1919, ibid., pp. 369–79.

5. Pinkerton report, 7 May 1920, Harvard Law School Library (hereafter HLS).

6. *The Sacco-Vanzetti Case*, supp. vol., pp. 9–10.

7. Thus, this exchange immediately before Bowles was asked about the shotgun bandit: "*Q.* Have you seen that man since, with the revolver? *A.* I am pretty positive I have. *Q.* Where? *A.* In the police station in this Court" (ibid., p. 18). The *Boston Herald*, 6 May 1920, stated that Bowles had identified both Sacco and Vanzetti.

8. *The Sacco-Vanzetti Case*, supp. vol., pp. 23–26.

9. Ibid., pp. 77–89.

10. Ibid., pp. 43–60.

11. Ibid., pp. 89–104.

12. Ibid., pp. 115–17.

13. Ibid., pp. 105, 126–27, 137.

14. Ibid., p. 150.

15. Pinkerton reports, 7, 10, 11 May 1920, HLS.

16. In fact, no one marked the shells for identification, and police officers could not therefore positively identify them at either trial. Other evidence suggests that the shells introduced in Dedham were not even the same as

those introduced in Plymouth. See Herbert Ehrmann, *The Case That Will Not Die* (Boston: Little, Brown, 1969), pp. 99–115, for a fuller discussion of the shotgun-shell evidence.

17. *The Sacco-Vanzetti Case*, supp. vol., pp. 141–42.

18. Ibid., p. 209. Ehrmann notes evidence that Proctor's testimony was not fully transcribed; the transcript of the Plymouth trial is incomplete, and jurors' affidavits, discussed below, suggest that he testified as to the shot in Vanzetti's shells.

19. Ibid., pp. 334–36; Ehrmann, *Case That Will Not Die*, pp. 108–9.

20. Ehrmann, *Case That Will Not Die*, pp. 108–14.

21. *The Sacco-Vanzetti Case*, supp. vol., pp. 149–63.

22. Ibid., pp. 142–44.

23. Ibid., p. 106.

24. Ibid., p. 163.

25. Ibid., pp. 193, 203.

26. Ibid., pp. 186–87, 370–71. Interestingly enough, Hassam's original description does bear a substantial resemblance to the original descriptions of the shotgun bandit.

27. Ibid., p. 333. The transcript of the charge is obviously incomplete, but the first paragraph of the printed charge deals with this issue.

28. See below, chap. 4.

Chapter 4

1. Brouillard had formerly been police chief of the town of Whitman. See *The Sacco-Vanzetti Case*, supp. vol., p. 193.

2. Grand Jury minutes, box 18, HLS. The defense never received any information whatsoever about the grand jury testimony. It is not uncommon for prosecutors to withhold some of their evidence in grand jury proceedings, but as we shall see when we consider the prosecution's development of its case, the evidence presented by Katzmann in September seems to have been the only evidence he had at that time.

3. The Southeastern District, for which Frederick Katzmann was the district attorney, included both Norfolk County, where the Dedham trial took place, and Plymouth County, where Vanzetti was tried.

4. The following analysis is based upon data from official court records: "Superior Criminal Court Docket, vols. 4–6," Dedham Courthouse, and "Records of the Superior Criminal Court" and "Cases of the Superior Criminal Court," Plymouth Courthouse. The authors thank the personnel of these two courthouses for their cooperation in making these records available.

5. This is the one area in which

the dockets are frequently inaccurate; while they are supposed to show counsel for the defense, the authors have found several cases in which no counsel is shown even though one was retained. Thus the figure of thirty-seven defendants represented is undoubtedly low, but one cannot say how low.

6. Depositions regarding Mrs. De Falco's approaches taken by Moore during the episode will be found under "De Falco, Anna," sv 203(6), BPL.

7. *Boston Globe*, 27 January through 4 February 1921. See also oral history interview by Aldino Felicani, 8 July 1954, copy in Herbert B. Ehrmann Papers, box 12, HLS.

8. The full facts of these cases will be found in 239 Massachusetts Cases, pp. 458 ff., and 240 Massachusetts Cases, pp. 240 ff.

9. Francis Russell, *Tragedy in Dedham* (New York: McGraw-Hill, 1962), pp. 121, 191.

10. *Boston Globe*, 1 and 3 February 1921, evening eds.

11. Ibid., 2 February 1921, morning ed.

12. "De Falco, Anna," sv 203(6), BPL.

13. G. S. Beamish, 5 March 1922, "William Dodson," sv 202–3, BPL.

14. See the affidavit of Fred J. Weyand, in *The Sacco-Vanzetti Case*, 5:4503, and below, chap. 11.

15. Ibid., p. 4493. Katzmann admitted that the interview had taken place but said he had simply told the man he had nothing for him to do (p. 4612).

16. *Boston Globe*, 2 February 1921, morning ed. Squires refused to discuss the case with Francis Russell shortly before his death in 1960 (Russell, *Tragedy in Dedham*, p. 121).

Chapter 5

1. Osmond K. Fraenkel, *The Sacco-Vanzetti Case* (New York: Alfred A. Knopf, 1931), pp. 205–330, gives the most thorough summary of the identification testimony available.

2. Pinkerton reports, 19, 20, 23 April 1920, HLS.

3. The authors have made several attempts to locate a photograph of Palmisano but without result.

4. "Identifications of Defendant Nicola Sacco," Harold Williams notebook, box 22, HLS.

5. Pinkerton reports, 6 and 7 May 1920, HLS.

6. Preliminary hearing, Sacco-Vanzetti Collection, box 18, HLS.

7. Grand Jury minutes, box 18, HLS.

8. *The Sacco-Vanzetti Case*, 1: 223–24, 252.

9. Pinkerton reports, 19 April and 11 May 1920, HLS.

10. "Identifications of Defendant Nicola Sacco," Williams notebook, box 22, HLS.

11. Ibid., box 18.

12. Ibid.

13. *The Sacco-Vanzetti Case*, 1:460–78.

14. Ibid., 2:2217.

15. Williams witness notebook, box 22, HLS.

16. *The Sacco-Vanzetti Case*, 1:292–97, 302–22.

17. Ibid., 2:1122–90.

18. Ibid., 5:5564–95.

19. Ibid., 1:332–52.

20. Ibid., 2:1373–85.

21. *Boston Globe*, 16 February 1921, evening ed., p. 2.

22. Massachusetts State Police files.

23. *The Sacco-Vanzetti Case*, 2:1308–12.

24. Ibid., 4:3896–960.

25. Ibid., 1:542–47.

26. Ibid., 4:3740.

27. Ibid., 2:1353, 1356, 1399, 1488.

28. Williams witness notebook, box 22, HLS.

29. See *The Sacco-Vanzetti Case*, 3:3733–887.

30. Williams witness notebook, box 22, HLS.

31. *The Sacco-Vanzetti Case*, 1:501.

32. Williams witness notebook, box 22, HLS.

33. *The Sacco-Vanzetti Case*, 1:518–40.

34. Ibid., supp. vol., pp. 441–42.

35. Pinkerton reports, 22 and 23 April 1920, HLS.

36. Ibid., 7 May.

37. Grand Jury minutes, box 18, HLS.

38. *The Sacco-Vanzetti Case*, supp. vol., pp. 204–19.

39. "Identifications of Defendant Bert Vanzetti," Williams notebook, box 22, HLS.

40. *The Sacco-Vanzetti Case*, supp. vol., p. 451.

41. Pinkerton report, 18 April 1920, HLS.

42. Ibid., 6 and 7 May.

43. *The Sacco-Vanzetti Case*, 1:413–25.

44. Ibid., 1:965; 2:2000.

45. Ibid., 2:2215.

46. Ibid., 1:437–39.

47. Ibid., 2:1275–98.

48. Grand Jury minutes, box 18, HLS.

49. *The Sacco-Vanzetti Case*, 1:594–616.

50. Ibid., pp. 488–97.

51. Dolbeare deposition, 8 June 1921, in Moore Papers, book J, BPL.

52. Pinkerton reports, 17, 20, 21 April 1920, HLS; *The Sacco-Vanzetti Case*, 1:1011; 2:1226.

53. *The Sacco-Vanzetti Case*, supp. vol., pp. 452–57.

54. De Forrest apparently did identify Orciani as one of the men

he saw; see the *Boston Herald*, 9 May 1920.

55. *The Sacco-Vanzetti Case*, 5:5415–16.

56. Ibid., supp. vol., pp. 396–98; 1:256–65.

57. Ibid., supp. vol., pp. 44–49; 1:278–88.

58. Ibid., 2:1190–208.

59. Ibid., pp. 1095–122.

60. Ibid., 4:3503.

61. Ibid., 1:969–77.

62. Ibid., 2:1212.

Chapter 6

1. *The Sacco-Vanzetti Case*, 2: 1743–802.

2. Ibid., p. 1753.

3. "Bert Vanzetti," Massachusetts State Police files.

4. *The Sacco-Vanzetti Case*, 2: 1905–46.

5. Ibid., pp. 1947–51.

6. "Nicola Sacco," Massachusetts State Police files.

7. Grand Jury minutes, p. 3, box 18, HLS.

8. *The Sacco-Vanzetti Case*, 5: 5042.

9. Ibid., p. 5232.

10. Massachusetts State Police files.

11. *The Sacco-Vanzetti Case*, 1:751–52.

12. Statement taken by M. E. Stewart, 19 May 1921, Massachusetts State Police files.

13. *The Sacco-Vanzetti Case*, 1:752–53.

14. Ibid., p. 780.

15. Grand Jury minutes, pp. 68–69, box 18, HLS.

16. Unsigned and undated notes, "Officer Connelly," SV 202–3, BPL.

17. *The Sacco-Vanzetti Case*, 2:2259–60.

18. Ibid., pp. 1710–11, 1810–11, 1848–49.

19. Edward Houlton James, "The Story of Mario Buda before the Jury of the World," HLS.

20. See below, chap. 12.

21. Robert Montgomery, *Sacco-Vanzetti: The Murder and the Myth* (New York: Devin-Adair, 1960), pp. 177–78, flirts with this point but apparently did not take the trouble to read the newspapers of 4 May in which the government specifically accused the Galleanisti of the bombings.

22. *The Sacco-Vanzetti Case*, 1:842–50; 2:2110–11.

23. Pernicone, "Carlo Tresca and the Sacco-Vanzetti Case."

24. 21 January 1921, Massachusetts State Police files.

25. Thompson to Charles B. Rogers, 19 November 1926, box 25, HLS.

26. For Thompson's original record, see the Sacco-Vanzetti Papers, box 17, folder 7, HLS. An almost complete version can be found in Herbert Ehrmann, *The*

Untried Case (New York: The Vanguard Press, 1933).

Chapter 7

1. The issue of the alibis has been very thoroughly treated. For fuller treatments, see Fraenkel, *Sacco-Vanzetti Case*, pp. 474–509, or Ehrmann, *Case That Will Not Die*, pp. 329–73.

2. *The Sacco-Vanzetti Case*, 2: 1494, 1522, 1586, 1548, 1585, 1674.

3. Ibid., pp. 1679, 1667, 1662, 1991, 1645, 2266a.

4. Murdulo statement, 12 April 1921, in Moore Papers, book C, BPL.

5. *The Sacco-Vanzetti Case*, 2: 2024, 2033.

6. Report of William West, 7 October 1919, Department of Justice file 9-12-276, National Archives. The list also includes one Palmira Boni of 10 North Square, Boston, apparently the proprietor of Boni's restaurant.

7. FBI file 61-126-176.

8. Pernicone, "Carlo Tresca and the Sacco-Vanzetti Case," p. 544.

9. Ehrmann, *Case That Will Not Die*, p. 367.

10. Ricci deposition, 25 January 1921, in Moore Papers, book I, BPL.

11. *The Sacco-Vanzetti Case*, 2: 1823, 1832.

12. Ibid., pp. 1979–81.

13. Ibid., 1:871–72.

14. "Nicola Sacco," Massachusetts State Police files.

15. Ehrmann, *Case That Will Not Die*, p. 383.

16. *The Sacco-Vanzetti Case*, 2: 1661.

17. Ibid., pp. 2033–52. To make his point, Katzmann had Affe reproduce the notation in the book on a piece of paper. The paper survives in Dedham Courthouse, but the authors have been unable to find the original notebook introduced by the defense.

18. Ibid., pp. 1365–71.

19. Ibid., pp. 2014–24.

20. Sinclair to Ehrmann, 16 June 1928, in Ehrmann Papers, box 14, HLS.

21. Moore Papers, book J, BPL.

Chapter 8

1. Williams in his opening statement said that the prosecution would also introduce a shotgun shell found near the car that would match some of the shells found on Vanzetti on the night of his arrest. The shell was never introduced. The reason, it is clear from the grand jury proceedings, is that a boy had found the shell "near where the car was found in the woods," and since the Manley Woods were a popular hunting

area, it was impossible to connect the shell to the car convincingly (Grand Jury minutes, p. 73, box 18, HLS).

2. *The Sacco-Vanzetti Case*, 2: 1629–44. On cross-examination Slater dated the sale "late in the fall. . . . Probably October or November."

3. John Dever Manuscript, BPL.

4. *The Sacco-Vanzetti Case*, supp. vol., p. 441. John Dever said he had been influenced by witnesses who claimed to have seen a "white gun" corresponding in color to Vanzetti's revolver sticking out of the getaway car as it drove away.

5. Ibid., p. 411.

6. Ibid., 1:196–99.

7. See the report by the insurance adjuster M. L. Hines, 22 April 1920, in Pinkerton reports, HLS.

8. "Dr. F. Russell Dame," Williams witness notebook, box 22, HLS.

9. Memorandum by M. E. Stewart, interview with Mrs. Alexander Berardelli, 31 January 1921; interview at Williams's office, 12 February 1921; memorandum by Stewart, 12 February 1921, Massachusetts State Police files. Changing her story at the trial, she said on cross-examination that Parmenter had given her husband another gun while the original one was in the shop (*The Sacco-Vanzetti Case*, 1:808–9).

10. Stewart memorandums, 12

and 15 February 1921, Massachusetts State Police files.

11. Stewart memorandum, 18 February 1921, Massachusetts State Police files.

12. *The Sacco-Vanzetti Case*, 5: 5234–38. Wadsworth also told the committee that he had in 1921 been working for the Department of Justice watching radicals.

13. See "List of Property held by Captain William H. Proctor in the Sacco and Vanzetti Case," n.d., Massachusetts State Police files.

14. Williams witness notebook, box 22, HLS.

15. *The Sacco-Vanzetti Case*, 2: 1686–87.

16. Ibid., 1:170, 196.

Chapter 9

1. *The Sacco-Vanzetti Case*, 1: 796–98, 854.

2. Stewart memorandum, 3 June 1921, Massachusetts State Police files.

3. "Fred Loring," SV 203(7), BPL.

4. *The Sacco-Vanzetti Case*, 5: 5178–79.

5. Another story about the cap is related by Montgomery, *Sacco-Vanzetti*, p. 117. Stewart apparently told Montgomery that he had taken a few hairs from a comb Sacco was using in jail and asked Dr. Magrath, the medical examiner of Suffolk County, to compare them with hairs found upon

the "Loring cap." According to Stewart, Magrath told him that they were "identical," but Katzmann declined to use the evidence in court, reportedly because he feared that the defense would make a telling pun on the idea of "hanging a man by a hair." Montgomery also claimed to have heard the same story from a friend of Magrath's.

This story, however, cannot for a variety of reasons be taken seriously. First of all, Stewart's memory frequently betrayed him in the decades following the case. More important, no record apparently existed that would have confirmed the origin of either the hairs from the cap or the hairs from the comb—and given Stewart's role in the preparation of much of the prosecution's fraudulent evidence, his word cannot be trusted. Last and most important, it is clear that Magrath's opinion—presuming that he even expressed one—cannot be taken seriously. The matching of human hairs is today recognized as a highly complex procedure involving the use of powerful comparison microscopes, a tool unavailable to Magrath, and the specification of about a hundred different variables. Even today the question of whether it is possible definitely to match hair specimens is hotly debated among forensic scientists. See B. D.

Gaudette and E. S. Keeping, "An Attempt at Determining Probabilities in Human Scalp Hair Comparison," *Journal of Forensic Sciences* 19, no. 3 (July 1974): 599–606; P. D. Barnett and R. R. Ogle, "Probabilities and Human Hair Comparisons," and B. D. Gaudette, "A Supplementary Discussion of Probabilities and Human Hair Comparisons," ibid., 27, no. 2 (April 1982): 272–89.

6. *The Sacco-Vanzetti Case*, 1: 884–93.

7. Ibid., 2:1432–35.

8. Montgomery, *Sacco-Vanzetti*, p. 98. For confirmation that all six of Sacco's bullets were of this type, see the affidavit of Albert Hamilton, in *The Sacco-Vanzetti Case*, 3:3634–35.

9. *The Sacco-Vanzetti Case*, 5: 5378w–78x.

10. Herbert B. Ehrmann, "Sacco and Vanzetti: The 'Magnetic Point' and the Morelli Evidence," *Harvard Law Review* 79, no. 3 (January 1966): 579–80.

11. Ehrmann, *Case That Will Not Die*, pp. 283–84.

12. *The Sacco-Vanzetti Case*, 5: 5225–28.

13. Russell, *Tragedy in Dedham*, p. 317.

14. See Judge Michael A. Musmanno, "The Sacco-Vanzetti Case," *University of Kansas Law Review* 11 (1963): 481–525.

15. Russell to Frank Giles, 10 July 1961, and John Collins to

Giles, 19 September 1961, Massachusetts State Police files.

16. Select Committee on Sacco and Vanzetti, "Examination of Firearm-Related Evidence: The Nicola Sacco and Bartolomeo Vanzetti Case" (copy in author's possession). David E. Kaiser thanks Professor James Starrs of George Washington University for making this copy available. The panel did conclude, based on photographs taken by a defense expert in the 1920s, that the bullet III now in possession of Massachusetts authorities is the same one examined during the 1920s.

17. Pinkerton report, 22 April 1920, HLS.

18. *The Sacco-Vanzetti Case*, supp. vol., pp. 440–44.

19. Ibid., 1:203.

20. Ibid., supp. vol., pp. 419–25.

21. Ibid., pp. 267–71.

22. Pinkerton report, 22 April 1920, HLS.

23. *The Sacco-Vanzetti Case*, 1: 188–93.

24. Ibid., pp. 98–137.

25. Ibid., pp. 100–3, 125, 135. Dr. Jones originally thought that the chest wound might have been fired from the left but changed his mind after the evidence of Parmenter's clothing showed that the bullet had entered in the center of his chest.

26. Ibid., pp. 112–18. The text of Dr. Magrath's testimony is occasionally confusing because he also numbered the wounds according to a different scheme; all numbers in this text refer to the numbers of the bullets.

27. At this point the accounts of other witnesses should be considered. Annie Nichols said at the inquest that, from inside her house about two hundred feet from the shooting, she saw a man chase Parmenter across the road and fire two shots at him. Like Bostock, she apparently thought that a bandit who followed Parmenter across the street to get his money box was firing a weapon. At the trial she altered her testimony and said she had also seen a man—perhaps the same one, perhaps not—step up to Berardelli and fire. See ibid., supp. vol., p. 397, and 1:257. While vague, this testimony does not directly contradict McGlone, Bostock, and Wade. Several other witnesses did give more contradictory accounts. Edward Carter, a shoe worker at Slater and Morrill, saw the shooting from a window over two hundred feet away. He said he saw a man step out of the car, walk up to Berardelli, and shoot him, after which Berardelli went down (supp. vol., p. 432). All other accounts agree that Berardelli was long since down when the car came up. Edgar Langlois and Sam Akeke watched from an upper-floor window in the Rice and

Hutchins factory. They had to open a window to see what was happening; after doing so, both claimed that they saw two men with automatics firing rapidly at Berardelli, one from in front of him and one from behind. These accounts cannot be reconciled either with the testimony of the three best-placed witnesses or, in many cases, with the firearms evidence, and they have a confused flavor very different from the precision of McGlone, Wade, and Bostock. Their observations are also questionable because of the time it took to open windows and because, as another witness admitted, the operation of the factories made a tremendous noise.

28. Ibid., 1:127.

29. Ehrmann, *Case That Will Not Die*, pp. 280–81, questions the authenticity of bullet III based on the eyewitness testimony. Fraenkel, *Sacco-Vanzetti Case*, p. 342, also noted that the eyewitness testimony is hard to reconcile with the uniqueness of bullet III. Neither one of them, however, made the link with the evidence of the autopsies.

30. *The Sacco-Vanzetti Case*, 1:194.

31. Grand Jury minutes, p. 69, box 18, HLS.

32. In *Tragedy in Dedham* and elsewhere, Francis Russell has repeatedly argued that no one connected with the prosecution would have fraudulently introduced shell w as evidence because, at that time, firearms experts did not realize that the breechblock markings on shells could not be used to identify the weapon from which they had been fired. This statement is false and misleading. Affidavits of 1923 by several firearms experts involved in the case show that they *did* know that breechblock markings could be used to identify shells. See *The Sacco-Vanzetti Case*, 4: 3571–72, 3625. The firearms experts who testified at the trial of Sacco and Vanzetti also attempted to identify the weapon from which shell w had been fired *in various other ways*—principally by measuring the indentation made by the firing pin and its location. It would have been perfectly logical for a prosecution investigator to substitute a shell as well as a bullet.

Chapter 10

1. Actually, as the defense brought out at the trial, at least one foreign automatic also produced bullets with a left twist.

2. *The Sacco-Vanzetti Case*, supp. vol., p. 414.

3. Grand Jury minutes, pp. 44, 46, 48, box 18, HLS. That Magrath turned the bullets over to Captain Proctor on 3 August is confirmed

by another document: "List of Property Held by Captain William H. Proctor in the Sacco and Vanzetti Case," n.d., Massachusetts State Police files.

4. See Luke G. Tedeschi, M.D., "George Burgess Magrath: Tribute to a Resting Lion," *American Journal of Forensic Medicine and Pathology* 1, no. 2 (June 1980): 169–72.

5. It should, however, be noted that according to several people who knew him Magrath was later persuaded that the ballistics evidence against Sacco was decisive.

6. Williams notebook, box 22, HLS. This notation was first discovered by Lincoln Robbins of Buzzard's Bay, Massachusetts; see Jackson, *Black Flag*, pp. 107–9.

7. Pinkerton report, 22 April 1920, HLS; "James Bostock," Williams witness notebook, box 22, HLS. There is no date on the latter statement, but virtually all the other statements in the file date from January or February 1921.

8. Pinkerton report, 22 April 1920, HLS.

9. *The Sacco-Vanzetti Case*, 1: 195, 882–83.

10. Robert Reid memorandum, 24 March 1924, in Moore Papers, book A, BPL.

11. See Williams's opening statement, in *The Sacco-Vanzetti Case*, 1:77.

12. "George B. Magrath," Williams witness notebook, box 22, HLS.

13. *The Sacco-Vanzetti Case*, 1: 118–20.

14. The date of Williams's handwritten notes is critical. These notes, now on deposit at the Manuscript Division of the Harvard Law School Library, are no longer bound in a loose-leaf notebook, although they have holes punched in the left-hand margin. They begin with descriptions of the identifications of Sacco and Vanzetti immediately after their arrest. Then follows a series of memorandums by Stewart, all written in late January and early February 1921. Next comes a typewritten outline of the Bridgewater and South Braintree cases. Two handwritten notes of interrogations by John Shay in late January 1921 follow. Then comes a long, undated list of witnesses; a note on the history of the bandit car; and a list of property held by Captain Proctor, which, though undated, could not possibly have been written before early January 1921, since it refers to transfers of exhibits on 3 January. The original descriptions of the bandits follow; then comes some correspondence written in early February 1921. Next come the handwritten notes that refer to the existence of a Colt bullet. Some of the notes seem to be based on the aforemen-

tioned list of exhibits held by Proctor. Then follows a long, undated typewritten outline. Everything in the notebook therefore suggests that the notes were prepared in late January or early February 1921, probably after 5 February, when a March trial date was first set.

15. *The Sacco-Vanzetti Case,* 1:923.

16. Ibid., p. 889.

17. In 1962 Shelley Braverman, a ballistics expert consulted by Herbert Ehrmann, fired a bullet of the type of bullet III into a one-inch board. The deformation produced by the firing was very similar to that of bullet III. Braverman, "Were Sacco and Vanzetti Framed?" *Guns Magazine,* May 1963, p. 16.

18. *The Sacco-Vanzetti Case,* 1:886.

19. Lowell Committee Papers, Harvard University Archives.

20. Montgomery, *Sacco-Vanzetti,* pp. 224–25.

21. *The Sacco-Vanzetti Case,* 5:5185–86.

22. Ibid., 1:895–97, 919–20.

23. Jack Disbrow Gunther and Charles O. Gunther, *Identification of Firearms from Ammunition Fired Therein with an Analysis of Legal Authorities* (New York, 1935), pp. 160–62.

24. Ibid., p. 160.

25. *The Sacco-Vanzetti Case,* 4:

3666–67; see also Gunther and Gunther, *Identification of Firearms,* pp. 231–39.

26. *The Sacco-Vanzetti Case,* 2: 2224–28, 2254.

27. Box 6, folder 5, HLS.

28. *The Sacco-Vanzetti Case,* 5:4977.

29. Ibid., 4:3641–43, 3681–82. Katzmann also filed an affidavit in response and stated that Proctor, "in the summer and fall of 1920," had examined the four Berardelli bullets, "and he informed me that three of the said bullets were, in his opinion, fired from a 32 calibre Savage automatic pistol, and the fourth of said bullets had been fired from a 32 calibre Colt automatic pistol" (p. 3681).

30. According to Thompson, Proctor did tell him about these episodes at the time he gave his affidavit but apparently refused to put them in writing (Ibid., 5:4539).

31. Ibid., p. 5085.

32. Ibid., 5:5037–85.

33. *Boston University Law Review* 26 (1946): 240–41. The reference to barrel-switching may well refer to a November 1923 episode involving a defense expert, Albert Hamilton; see Russell, *Tragedy in Dedham,* pp. 247–49.

Chapter 11

1. *The Sacco-Vanzetti Case*, 5: 4500–7.

2. BI, OG 20713.

3. "Summary Report in re Bomb Explosions of June 2, 1919," FBI file 61-5-407.

4. BS 202600–22.

5. *New York Times*, 17–19 September 1920.

6. C. J. Scully, "Memorandum for W. J. Flynn," 18 October 1920, FBI file 61-5-203.

7. "Radical Activities in the Boston District," 25 September 1920, BS 206200–22.

8. BI, OG 360257.

9. Boston report of 15 October 1920, and Charles Hanrahan to Flynn, 16 and 22 October 1920, FBI files 61-5-174, 207, 217, 218.

10. West to Hoover, 15 August 1927, FBI file 61-126.

11. BS 202600–418.

12. Hill report, 10 February 1921, BS 202600–418.

13. Report of 16 November 1920, BS 202500–22.

14. BS 211205–224 et seq.

15. BS 211205.

16. BS 202600–418.

17. For these reports, see BS 202600–418.

18. BS 202600–418.

19. See FBI file 61-126.

20. Dowd to Hoover, 8 July 1926, FBI file 61-126.

21. Ibid.

22. Dowd to Hoover, 17 July 1926, FBI file 61-126.

23. J. Edgar Hoover, "Memorandum for the Files," 8 August 1927, FBI file 61-126.

24. See above, chap. 2.

25. BI, OG 360257.

26. Approached by Thomas O'Connor, a defense attorney, on 22 August 1927, Hill denied that he had ever worked on the Sacco-Vanzetti case. This was false; his report on the De Falco trial survives. See National Archives, Department of Justice, file 202600–418.

27. FBI file 61-126-790.

28. FBI file 61-126-176.

29. "Telephone Statement by A. L. Becker, July 7, 1921," Dedham Courthouse.

30. *The Sacco-Vanzetti Case*, 2:1944.

31. Ibid., 5:5042.

32. Ibid., 2:1629.

33. Ibid., 5:5059–60, 5081.

34. Francis Russell, "End of a Myth," *National Review*, 19 August 1977, states that drinking on the job had been one reason for their dismissal. Passages relating to their conduct were deleted from the copy of the FBI files on the case supplied to the authors.

Chapter 12

1. The Plympton Foundry where Orciani worked had a time clock but did not save time cards.

The pay records based on the time cards showed that Orciani had missed only one day in the week of 20–27 December 1920—Christmas, obviously—and that he had worked a full week the week of 15 April. See defense investigator Reid's memorandum on conversations with the factory owner and foreman, 17 May 1921, Ehrmann Papers, box 6, HLS.

2. *The Sacco-Vanzetti Case,* 5:5082.

3. Quoted in Cook, "The Missing Fingerprints."

4. D'Attilio, "La Salute è in Voi," p. 86.

5. Ibid., pp. 85–86.

6. Memorandums of interviews with George Kisirian, 15 December 1920, and Mr. and Mrs. Dolbec, 27 March 1921, Ehrmann Papers, box 6, HLS.

7. *The Sacco-Vanzetti Case,* 5: 5160–61.

8. Moore Papers, book H, BPL.

9. James, "The Story of Mario Buda."

10. Russell, *Tragedy in Dedham,* p. 295n.

11. *The Sacco-Vanzetti Case,* 1: 725–28.

12. See "Ferruccio Coacci, alias, Eriole Correcca," "Coacci's Trunk," and "Ferruccio Coacci," n.d., Massachusetts State Police files.

13. This according to Bostock, who carried Parmenter into a neighboring house; Pinkerton report, 22 April 1920, HLS.

14. Ehrmann Papers, box 6, HLS.

15. Di Lillo report, 4 April 1921, FBI file 61-5, 211204-501. On Malatesta, see Paul Avrich, "Italian Anarchism in America: An Historical Background to the Sacco-Vanzetti Case," in *Sacco-Vanzetti: Developments and Reconsiderations,* pp. 61–67.

16. For Vanzetti's letters, see SV 7B, BPL. David Kaiser thanks Krystyna von Henneberg for her help in translating these letters.

17. Russell, "End of a Myth," pp. 540 ff; *The Sacco-Vanzetti Case,* 2:2074. The FBI deleted specific information on the New York office's reply from the files it furnished to the present writers.

18. Boston office report, 6 December 1921, FBI file 61-126-434; Defense Papers, box 16-3, folder B-15, HLS, includes a photograph of Dodson.

19. "William Dodson," SV 202–3, BPL.

20. Russell, *Tragedy in Dedham,* introduction to the fiftieth-anniversary edition, p. xx, suggests the extraordinary theory that Dodson was the fifth man in the car together with Boda, Coacci, Orciani, and Sacco. Neither the federal authorities nor the defense investigators turned up any evidence that Dodson knew any Italian anarchists, and his wife specifically quoted him as saying that the

police were all wrong about Sacco and Vanzetti.

21. "Berardelli, Alexander," sv 202–3, BPL.

22. "Frederick Webster," sv 208–9, BPL.

23. "Memoranda in re Mrs. Sarah Berardelli," "Alexander Berardelli," sv 202–3, BPL.

24. Stewart memorandum, 4 February 1921, Massachusetts State Police files. Mrs. Berardelli changed her story completely when Katzmann interviewed her not long afterward.

25. The Sacco-Vanzetti Case, 5: 4661, 4400, 4472–74.

26. New York Times, 11 and 13 February, 14 August 1921.

27. These identifications, coming years after the crime, are inevitably suspect.

28. See Madeiros's affidavit, 29 May 1926, and his deposition, 28 June, in The Sacco-Vanzetti Case, 5:4416–17, 4615–718.

29. Thomas Driver later confirmed his acquaintance with Madeiros. He said he had not seen the car—he thought he had been in school at the time—but that he thought his mother, now deceased, had seen it (ibid., pp. 4559–660).

30. Ibid., supp. vol., p. 455.

31. Ibid., p. 452; Pinkerton report, 17 April 1920, HLS.

32. The Sacco-Vanzetti Case, supp. vol., pp. 426–27, 438–40.

33. Boston Globe, 17 April 1920, morning ed.

34. The Sacco-Vanzetti Case, 1:138–42.

35. Ehrmann Papers, box 14-8, HLS. Neal's memory seems to have failed him regarding his own attitude before the trial. In November 1920 he refused to talk to a defense investigator and added, "Anything I can do to convict them I will do" (Woodbury memorandum, 24 November 1920, in Moore Papers, book H, BPL).

36. Ehrmann, The Case That Will Not Die, pp. 416–17. King could fix the time of the car's arrival in Matfield precisely because it coincided with the passage of a particular train.

37. The Sacco-Vanzetti Case, 5:4586–87.

38. Ehrmann, The Untried Case, pp. 44–47.

39. Unfortunately, in their excitement at finding the car, the police do not seem to have tried to establish whether anyone failed to find it in the Manley Woods on 16 April.

40. "Identification," n.d., in Moore Papers, book H, BPL.

41. Testimony of Carl Knips, in The Sacco-Vanzetti Case, supp. vol., p. 458. Francis Devlin also testified at the preliminary hearing that there had been no number plate on the back (Preliminary Hearings, box 18, HLS).

42. The Sacco-Vanzetti Case, 1:

573–84. Clark did not definitely say that he saw the number plate on the back, but he said that he had never seen the front of the car, only the side and the rear. Kelliher at the grand jury told Katzmann she had gotten the number from the rear. At the trial she said she had gotten some from the front and some from the rear, a distortion all too typical of the prosecution's numerous efforts to make evidence square with its case (pp. 590–94).

43. Ben H. Bagdikian, "New Light on Sacco and Vanzetti," *New Republic*, 13 July 1963.

44. See Russell, *Tragedy in Dedham*, pp. 313–14, and Ehrmann, "Sacco and Vanzetti," p. 592.

45. Vincent Terese with Thomas C. Renner, *My Life in the Mafia* (Greenwich: Fawcett Books, 1974), p. 57.

46. Russell, *Tragedy in Dedham*, p. 323; author's interview with Francis Moriarity, 23 March 1983; author's interview with Mrs. Sarah Ehrmann, 23 March 1983.

47. Russell, *Tragedy in Dedham*, pp. 107–16.

48. *The Sacco-Vanzetti Case*, 5:4991, 5050.

49. Ibid., pp. 4991, 5052.

50. Ibid., pp. 4981, 4991–92.

51. Moore was particularly interested in tentative confessions by Jimmy Mede and Frank Silva, two East Boston men, that they had planned the Bridgewater holdup attempt and that Silva had committed it with "Doggy" Bruno, "Guinea" Oates, and Joe Sammarco. In 1922 Moore went to the Atlanta Federal Penitentiary to try to secure an admittedly false confession from Silva, then serving time under the name of Paul Martini. He failed, but in 1928 Silva sold an article to *Outlook* confessing his role. More than thirty years later Joe Sammarco, who had spent more than thirty years in Charlestown State Prison for killing a policeman in a dance hall, told Francis Russell that there was not a word of truth to this story and, according to John Conrad, passed a lie detector test on this point. See Russell, *Tragedy in Dedham*, pp. 270–78, 318–25.

52. Upton Sinclair, "The Fishpeddlar and the Shoemaker," *Institute of Social Studies Bulletin* 2 no. 2 (Summer 1953).

53. Pernicone, "Carlo Tresca and the Sacco-Vanzetti Case."

54. Ibid.

55. "Tresca, Carlo," sv 203(6), BPL.

56. Pernicone has found that Tresca never expressed doubts as to Sacco's innocence to any Italians.

Chapter 13

1. Tom O'Connor, "The Origins of the Sacco-Vanzetti Case," *Vanderbilt Law Review* 14, no. 3 (June 1961): 993.

2. Reid memorandum, n.d., in Moore Papers, book F, BPL.

3. Memorandum of 6 January 1921, in Moore Papers, book E, BPL.

4. Moore Papers, book D, folio 445, BPL.

5. While it is true that the defense, rather than the prosecution, initially put the defendants' beliefs in evidence in order to explain their conduct on 5 May, Katzmann undoubtedly did take advantage of the opportunity to put their radical beliefs and their evasion of the draft in the worst possible light, especially in dealing with Sacco. See Fraenkel, *Sacco-Vanzetti Case*, pp. 429–57.

6. George Hinkley Lyman, *The Story of the Massachusetts Committee of Public Safety* (Boston, 1919), p. 52. The authors attempted to discover whether any of the men connected with the prosecution had belonged during the war to the American Protective League, which hunted down radicals and draft dodgers in 1917–19. Unfortunately, the Massachusetts records of the league have been destroyed.

7. "Harry W. Schwartz, Statement taken by M. E. Stewart May 19, 1921," Massachusetts State Police files.

8. *Brockton Enterprise*, 15 July 1921, quoted in Ehrmann, *Case That Will Not Die*, p. 273.

9. Van Amburgh to Sullivan, 14 April 1950, Massachusetts State Police files.

10. *New York Times*, 1 February 1978.

Index